Prologue

The notion of atrocities in U. S. WWII POW camps appears shocking and incredulous. That is likely to be the typical reader's reaction after completing Chapter I of *"An Ironic Point of Light."* Most people in the United States have never heard this story. The obvious questions are likely to occur to most readers: "Why have I never heard this before? With all of the investigative reporting that has resulted in national headlines during the past two decades, how could such a major story remain undetected?"

The answers to these questions began to unfold in a copy of the *The Twin Cities Reader—Book Review*, November 18, 1989. The headline for this review by Adam Platt was "The U. S. Contribution to the Annals of War Atrocities." The book being reviewed was *Other Losses* by James Bacque. On February 24, 1991, the *New York Times* included a book review entitled, "Ike and the Disappearing Atrocities" by Stephen Ambrose, Director of the Eisenhower Center at the University of New Orleans.

Both Platt and Ambrose report criticisms (1) of the number reported by Bacque—1 million German soldiers and civilians died as prisoners in camps run by the U.S. and France between April 1945 and January 1946, and (2) of Bacque attributing the primary blame to General Dwight D. Eisenhower.

What is most significant is that both reviewers commend Bacque for his discoveries and appear to accept, as accurate, the atrocities that are chronicled in *Other Losses*. Ambrose states, "Our first conclusion was that Mr. Bacque made a major historical discovery. There was widespread mistreatment of German prisoners in the spring and summer of 1945. Men were beaten, denied water, forced to live in open camps without shelter, given inadequate food rations and inadequate medical care. Their mail was withheld. In some casees prisoners made a 'soup' of water and grass in order to deal with their hunger. Men did die needlessly and inexcusably. This must be confronted, and it is to Mr. Bacque's credit that he forces us to do so."

In the same article, Ambrose stated, "Mr. Bacque makes a point that is irrefutable: some American G.I.'s and their officers were capable of acting in almost as brutal a manner as the Nazis. He has challenged us to reopen the question, to do the research required, to get at the full truth."

In the *New York Times*, in a letter to the editor on April 14, 1991, Martin Brech, Mahopac, N.Y., a U.S. prison guard at Andernach on the Rhine reinforced Bacque's findings with personal testimony. "(Ambrose) focuses only on the alledged food shortage. He doesn't address the other deprivations: were there also tent, blanket, clothing, medical and mailman shortages? There was certainly no water shortage; we were right on the Rhine, yet we denied the prisoners sufficient water. Maddened with thirst, some of them crawled under the wires and ran toward the river in open fields in broad daylight while American guards machine-gunned them. A friend in the camp kitchen showed me our abundant supplies and admitted we could feed the prisoners more. When I threw some of my surplus rations over the wires to them, I was threatened with imprisonment. I protested to my officers, and they said the starvation diet was ordered by 'higher ups' and was general policy."

First published in Canada, *Other Losses* was virtually unheard of in this country, having been rejected by 40 American publishers, according to Platt in the 1989 review. The book has since been published by St. Martin's Press, New York, N.Y., 1992.

Included in Platt's review was a devastating account by ex-prisoner, George Weiss. "We couldn't even lie down properly. All night we had to sit up jammed against each other. But the lack of water was the worst thing of all. We would drink our own urine. It tasted terrible, but what

An Ironic Point Of Light

Biography

The Story of a German
From Russia
Who Survived An
American World War II
Prisoner of War Camp

by Berneda J. Koller

Copyright © 1994 by
BERNEDA J. KOLLER

Library of Congress
Catalog Card Number 94-96015

ISBN 0-9640004-0-7

Printed in United States of America

PINE HILL PRESS, INC.
Freeman, S. Dak. 57029

Table of Contents

	Dedication to Reuben Goertz	iv
	Acknowledgments	v
	Prologue	vii
	Foreword	xi
	Introduction	xiii
Chapter I	The Capture	1
Chapter II	The French Connection	13
Chapter III	The Forming of the Man	17
Chapter IV	The Not So Great Escape	29
Chapter V	Slave Labor	31
Chapter VI	Lilly	35
Chapter VII	Leaving Bessarabia	47
Chapter VIII	Willi Winger and Lilly Mayer Meet...	49
Chapter IX	Going To Be A Soldier	53
Chapter X	On the Road Again	61
Chapter XI	Farewell To Arms	71
Chapter XII	Reunion and Repair	75
Chapter XIII	Shaping Up and Shipping Out	79
Chapter XIV	Beginnings in Bismarck	85
Chapter XV	Life As Citizens of America	91
Chapter XVI	Building A Business	99
Chapter XVII	Hurts and Healings	103
	Author's Notes	111
	Chronological References	113
	Bibliography	117
	Appendix	119

iii

Dedicated
to Reuben Goertz

— who escorted me to the chambers of my German-Russian ancestry and

— who accompanied my faltering ego just long enough for it to believe it could write a book.

Too much Bacque garbage. Not very good historically. P.

Acknowledgments

My mother's people were Germans from Russia who came to America in 1874. They live within my creative processes by which this project has been produced. I am grateful for the opportunities their decisions have provided. Through interest in my ancestral heritage I met Dr. Harry Delker who introduced me to Willi and Lilly Winger. It was he who recognized the significance of Willi's experience and encouraged me to write it. I thank him heartily for the hours of work and advice that he contributed to this project.

I am grateful to Margie Garner who skillfully edited the first primitive and also the final drafts; to Joni Thomas, as a comrade in creativity, who contributed to the front and back covers her artistic talent; to Mary Wagner, an English teacher of the highest caliber, who shaped and sharpened whatever innate skills I have; and to Tim Waltner, editor of the *Freeman Courier*, who printed my short stories for three years where I developed the courage to expose myself in print. Shirley Hart saved hours of work by transferring to me mega amounts of computer time and tips.

Without the gift of love this project would not have been possible. For those who gave it there will be rewards.

All of these people are Dakotans. We live where pioneer individualism forged the paths we tread. Each of our visions is recognized as a tiny, but important, fragment of the collective consciousness that represents democracy, where we believe in the right of free and individual expression.

2 Feb 1995

At the end of WWII we retained few German POWs.
Those retained were S.S. Troops and others suspected of War Crimes.
This might account for the Harsh Treatment — IF ANY.
          H Pople
I don't buy into BACQUE'S STORY.

else could we do? Some men got down on the ground and licked the ground to get some moisture. I was so weak I was already on my knees, when we finally got a little water to drink...But the Rhine was just outside the (fence). The guards sold us water through the (fence)...I saw thousands dying. They took the bodies away on trucks."

Bacque states in *Other Losses,* "Eisenhower had deplored the Germans' useless defense because of the waste of life. But Germans were dying far faster now that they had surrendered than they had during the war. *At least 10 times as many Germans died in the French and American camps as were killed in all the combat on the western front in north-west Europe from June 1941 to April 1945."* (pg. 64, 1991 Canadian edition)

Bacque also reported that, "According to stories told by ex-prisoners in Rheinberg to this day, the last act of the Americans at Rheinberg before the British took over in mid-June was to bulldoze one section of the camp level while there were still living men in their holes in the ground. Nothing of this has ever been known outside of the stories of the prisoners, which have taken 44 years to reach print." (pg. 135, 1991 Canadian edition)

Platt reported, "There are no similar reports from the prison camps of the Canadians, British, and Dutch, who refused to convert their POW camps into starvation and disease pens that the Americans oversaw, according to Bacque. The French camps did suffer high mortality, but they neither refused aid nor kept inspectors away as the United States did. Many of those who died in French camps had been transferred, near death, from American camps."

An admonition in the Publisher's Note of the St. Martin's edition, 1992, seems most appropriate: "We have lived in the shadow of World War II for so long that we've grown accustomed to seeing only the inhumanity of the enemy. Thus, we were able to live with the comforting idea that because our cause was noble, our actions, too, were largely beyond reproach... In a free society, the truth must be exposed, regardless of the consequences—especially if we don't like to hear it."

After reviewing the contents of the cited references, the reader of *An Ironic Point of Light* will know that Willi Winger's story has historical significance.

> Harry A. Delker, Ph.D.
> Aberdeen, South Dakota
> December 1993

Other Losses, James Bacque, General Paperbacks, 30 Lesmill Road, Toronto, Canada M3B 2T6, 1991; ISBN 0-7736-7309-1.

Other Losses, James Bacque, St. Martin's Press; 175-5th Ave. Room 1715; NY, NY 10010, 1992. ISBN 1-55058-173-5.

The Twin Cities Reader—Book Review, "The U.S. Contribution to the Annals of War Atrocities," by Adam Platt; Winter, 1989.

The *New York Times—Book Review,* "Ike and the Disappearing Atrocities," by Stephen E. Ambrose, February 25, 1991.

The *New York Times—Book Review,* letters to the editor, regarding "Ike and the Disappearing Atrocities," April 14, 1991.

Foreword

My first meeting with Willi and Lilly Winger occurred at their Bismarck, North Dakota, home in October, 1986. I was pursuing family history information. (Lilly's paternal grandmother and my maternal grandmother were sisters. I had published a family history, "The Bertsch Book—222 Years," in 1985 and was developing family charts involving my grandmother's brothers and sisters.)

As I completed genealogical notations about the Wingers' children and Lilly's parents, Willi began talking about his life. As he described his experiences as a German soldier and an American prisoner of war, I immediately appreciated the significance of this story. In addition to the fact that this was a dramatic story, it occurred to me that (to the best of my knowledge) this type of story involving an American POW in World War II had not been published.

Willi indicated that he would consent to having this story written. Convinced that I was not the most appropriate person to write this unique story, I began a search for someone who might be willing to undertake this project.

After reading a series of newspaper articles which my friend, Berneda Koller, had written for the *Freeman Courier* (a weekly newspaper in Freeman, South Dakota), I began to appreciate Bernie's style and her skills in formulating an interesting story. I discussed the idea of a book with Bernie. In February, 1989, Bernie accompanied me to Bismarck. I introduced Bernie to Willi and Lilly. For two days we pursued details of the Wingers' experiences. We made tape recordings and completed extensive notes. This was the genesis of a collaborative effort that resulted in a story contained in the pages of this book.

I was very appreciative of the gracious hospitality during my several visits to the Winger home, and I am delighted that many people will now have the opportunity to read about their unusual experiences.

I would like to extend a special "Thank You" to Bernie Koller for accepting my challenge and my sincere congratulations for completing a project which required patience, persistence, and personal sacrifices.

Harry A. Delker, Ph. D.
Aberdeen, South Dakota

Introduction
An Ironic Point of Light

The Story of a German from Russia who survived an American World War II prisoner of war camp

The world is still in a state of combined awe and shock that the Kremlin has crumbled. The collective blaze that burned communism began with individual flames for democratic rights. It is a reminder of a 20th Century electrician from a shipyard in Poland who convinced his fellow workers that they deserved better treatment. Solidarity rose up and cried for justice. Lech Walensa and each of his supporters made a difference.

Knowing that individual aspiration never goes out of style, George Bush encouraged each United States citizen to stretch beyond himself to volunteer service in his "Thousand Points of Light" speech in 1988.

W. Averell Harriman expressed this so eloquently with the help of British poet W. H. Auden in the *Twentieth Century: An Almanac (1984)*:

> Perhaps the greatest revolution of our time is not in the technology which can demolish or dehumanize us, but in the awakening of political consciousness among billions of men and women on all continents whom illiteracy, disease, hunger, and hopelessness had once doomed to apathy and irrelevance. Now they too are participants in the global search for dignity, for justice, and for a secure new order. It is a stumbling search, but it goes on and may yet produce marvels. What animates it is not collective madness but individual aspiration. In the absence of a solid center,

we still retain innate decency. Or as W. H. Auden, another great British poet, wrote on the eve of World War II:

> Defenceless under the night
> Our world in stupor lies:
> Yet dotted everywhere,
> Ironic points of light
> Flash out wherever the just
> Exchange their messages;
> May I, composed like them
> Of Eros and of dust,
> Beleaguered by the same
> Negation and despair,
> Show an affirming flame.

That 'affirming flame' continues to burn in hearts around the world. It is the energy which lights the way ahead.*

The following is a story about a German from Russia and his family whose life together was not destined to be a "marvel" for all the world to see, but rather a small and "ironic point of light." After an odyssey that covered five countries in Europe prior to and during World War II, this family brought its luminescence, a blend of mixed ideologies, to rest with the torch of liberty in America. The message is that the dignity of the individual is and must always remain important. The opportunity for a fit way to live is a precious commodity. As the world moves into the next century it is imperative that the search for decency continues to be "an affirmative flame — the energy which lights the way ahead."

*Reprinted with permission from Random House from W. H. Auden: Collected Poems by W. H. Auden, edit. by E. Mendelson, c1976.

Chapter I

The Capture

As the sound of a vehicle in the distance reached his ears, Willi shifted the weight of the rifle he was carrying from his left hand to his right. He turned to look back along the road on which he had been walking and rested his aching left foot. Though it was not a serious wound, Willi's sore foot had prevented him from keeping pace with his retreating German comrades. The bad news had been that his slower pace separated him from his unit. The good news had been that it gave him the opportunity to rest at moments of his choosing, and so he had chosen to stop at a farm along the way. The farm family had been sympathetic and provided him with food, civilian clothing, and a warm place to sleep and rest. During this respite from war-time duties, newscasters on the radio had reported that World War II had officially ended. Willi's farmer friend then made a suggestion.

"The war is over anyhow, now. They say on the loudspeaker to bring in all weapons to town. Would you like to take my gun for hunting and take it in there? It's only three miles."

Willi had agreed and now here he was . . . listening to the sound of an engine in the distance. It was coming nearer. The tiny apprehensions swimming around in his chest attacked his heart like a school of piranha when he saw it was an American jeep. He was sure the four American soldiers in it could hear the savage feeding frenzy occurring in his chest as they slammed on the brakes, jumped out, and surrounded him with shouts and gestures for him to surrender. Willi relinquished the rifle, it wasn't his anyway. He put his hands up on his head. He wanted to put them on his chest to warm and soothe what was left of his ravaged heart. It hurt.

Although Admiral Friedeburg and General Jodl had already signed the unconditional surrender of Germany at General Eisenhower's headquarters in a small schoolhouse in Reims, France, there was no indication here where Willi stood that World War II was over. There were four hostile rifles pointed at him. Willi climbed into the jeep that was covered with muck from the German countryside and attempted to explain,

"I was just taking this gun to town."

Not one of his custodians could speak German. Even though he was 24 years old, he felt as if he were a small boy caught with his hand in the cookie jar. He chastized himself.

"No papers to show I was born in Rumania, no money. no nothing. I don't even know how stupid I am. You never learn enough. This is the end of everything!"

Actually, it was the beginning. It was the first step of a long and arduous journey to the United States where Willi would spend the most productive years of his life laboring in a system he had been trained to fight in his youth.

Willi shook his head at his own mistaken judgement. If he hadn't been so lazy and had dug a respectable foxhole, maybe he wouldn't be in such a fix. Ten days ago his outfit had received orders to dig in because the Americans were on their way. His training as a German infantry interpreter had not prepared him for the resistance he found in the soil on that hill in West Germany, somewhere near Bad Homburg. So two and a half hours later when the American tanks arrived, his inadequate efforts had produced a foxhole too small for his entire frame. Choosing to protect his head, Willi's exposed left foot had made a good target for an American bullet resulting in a superficial but irritating wound. But now, the wound was in his chest. A primitive, cannibalistic urge arose from his depths wishing the piranha ripping at his center could continue to feast on him so that he would disappear . . . rip, rip, zip, nothing left to face the enemy.

"Didn't these guys know nothing? The radio had said operations were to cease May 8." It was May 15, 1945, and Wachtmeister Willi Winger had just been introduced to the United States of America. There was nothing in this tableau that suggested the admirable and cherished relationship that would ensue from this introduction.

One American jabbed the air with his weapon indicating for Willi to get into the vehicle and sit. Willi obeyed with sour thoughts.

"All my papers back there in the uniform at the farm. Where are they taking me? These guys didn't even listen that I'm on my way to the authorities with this gun. The war is done a few days ago, but here I go to visit the enemy. Too bad it was not my head instead of my foot that shook hands with America in that foxhole!"

The jeep was heading in the general direction of Frankfurt. They passed a sign that said Bad Kreuznach.

As the vehicle slowed and the dust cleared Willi saw in the distance what resembled heat waves emanating from what appeared to be huge chunks of dirty, lumpy tarp cast about carelessly on the ground with a fence surrounding the whole works as far as his eye could see. Drawing nearer, he recognized the fenced-in mass to be people – prisoners, dull and gloomy, milling around in the unseasonably hot temperature for May, clad in what was left of combat fatigues mixed with civilian clothing in bizarre combinations. The effects of the 100 degree temperature with no protection from the sun were obvious in the faces and postures of those men closest to the gate where the jeep entered. Before Willi was escorted to the American military commander in charge, he saw some cows in the distance. The incongruity of the scene brought a suppressed chuckle from his dry throat. What a pastoral picture – men and cows penned up together!

Willi was impressed with the man in charge. He could speak German and was friendly. He offered Willi some chocolate and they visited. Willi allowed himself a glimmering of hope. Maybe this guy would let him go. The man asked Willi how old he was and how long he had been in the German infantry. When Willi told how he had been within ten feet of Hitler during a dress parade in 1942, the man was curious and asked various other questions about Hitler, none of which Willi could answer. The conversation jumped around. This guy didn't seem to be in any hurry. Soon they were talking about America. Willi began to feel more expansive and volunteered additional information.

"Ya, my wife has relatives in South Dakota of the United States. Someday, maybe we go there."

As Willi munched his chocolate he told the story of his job as interpreter in the German army and how he came to be wounded in the foot and why he was on the road to town with the farmer's rifle.

In German the man asked how many languages Willi could speak. Willi's reply was four — German and Russian from his childhood environment, Rumanian from his early school days, and French from teacher's college.

Willi suspected that this commander was Jewish and later these suspicions were confirmed by information in the camp. However, it was years later before Willi spent any time reflecting about the significance of this commander being a German Jew. But now, Willi could see this officer had no intention of releasing anyone. Further attempts along these lines would be useless. The commander dismissed his newest captive to others.

Besides the rifle, the Americans took away whatever possessions Willi had, including his wedding ring, engagement ring and watch, leaving him with only the clothes on his back. A guard pointed for Willi to join the crowd; two other guards literally threw him into the compound. What was left of his hurting heart plummeted. Willi found a place for himself in the wide open pasture which served as a hastily constructed prisoner compound. There was one large tent in the center some distance from the gate. The reality of his situation was clear to him. The thousands of filthy faces and bodies before him revealed the lack of water for washing and the few eyes that turned to him briefly were blank and bleak. There was no grass. The bare ground looked merciless.

Willi assumed that some of the grimy faces and foul bodies he was gazing at were those he had seen some days earlier being picked up from their own lawns and homes near Bad Homburg. German women and children had been stunned as they watched their husbands, brothers, and sweethearts arrested. The war was supposed to be over. If the war was over, how could people be confiscated like property? When would this madness end? Willi had felt sick that day, but today he was numb as if injected with novocaine... anesthetized inside and out... except for his eyes.

It seemed to Willi that some participants in the hostilities of war enjoyed the opportunity to inflict unnecessary cruelty, indiscriminately, no matter what color uniform they wore. He had observed it many times in the last three or four years of this war. He thought,

"No one nationality was better or worse. Every unit had its war mongers." He sighed and shook his head.

Willi recalled one Sunday when he had been walking the same highway where the American soldiers had just picked him up. That Sunday it had seemed as if he were in a movie. It was a war scene and Willi was center stage.

"I had to go to another town. There I was and one American plane came down. On just myself they were shooting one hundred, maybe two hundred, shots. I was lucky. There was a forest. I could run into there so they would not get me. It was the American plane for one person. It did not mean a damn thing to them. The American pilots were the biggest criminals in the world... on the highway, on the street. They thought everybody was Nazi."

Willi knew the war was not over for him or the strangers in the squalor around him. What a fool he had been to believe that sweet talk on the radio. He felt as if he were about to be consumed... absorbed by this noisy, unwholesome, camouflaged-colored "amoeba" of a P.O.W. camp. He sighed as he allowed the bleakness of the Bad Kreuznach situation to suck him up.

"The Americans want prisoners. It does not matter anything to them. They still don't believe me a damn thing that I was taking the rifle to town."

He found a spot to sit and submerged himself into reflection and spent the next four days waiting for a drink of water. One, two, three... four days.

When a barrel of water did appear, Willi thought perhaps he might be imagining it. He didn't verbalize his thoughts for fear of his dry tongue crumbling to ashes with the effort. A draft of the tepid liquid renewed his parched mouth and then another washed four days of dirt and dust down his throat. He savored a sip by holding the precious moisture on his tongue, moving the water around like mouthwash. Never, never, never would he take for granted again the lovely, lively feel of water filling his throat and mouth... so sweet, so soft, so rejuvenating. But behind that momentary satisfaction lurked his consciousness for food. And now with his cells no longer keening for water, the hunger locked deep in the cellar of his psyche burst forth in full force like a gigantic Cyclops intent on its prey... only to find its dinner already devoured by some other invisible competitor. There was no dinner. There was no prey. But the gargantuan creature continued to hulk within Willi and silently growl. Willi attempted to think of other things, like Lilly, his bride of six months left behind in Poland. He took another swallow of water; just a sip was a luxury.

When his thirst was satiated, Willi felt refreshed enough to notice a passing truck loaded with bodies for whom the barrel of water held no significance. Momentarily renewed, he stood up. At least their troubles were over.

At least their stomachs were at rest. In resignation, he sat down again, heavily, on the bare, unsympathetic earth. He sighed and attempted to keep his 24-year-old spirit from feeling like a 100-year-old burden. He massaged the mark under his arm that designated his blood type as A. He had a tendency to do that when he felt vulnerable. It reminded him of his heritage. The blue imprint of numbers and letters had been imposed on all Rumanian refugees entering Germany in the early stages of the war. Each person, even children age two and up, had been tattooed with his or her blood type. Genetic certification of each family had been required by the German government. The process insured the screening of undesirable people and provided documentation of blood for war-time transfusions. All Nazi Secret Service personnel were likewise stamped, although Willi was not aware of this fact at this time in his life. But now, as Willi touched his arm, his Rumanian childhood which had offered so much security in the past seemed like a fantasy and held no assurance for him in this prison camp.

It helped when cans of spinach were distributed... at least for a few days. Soon it became apparent that spinach was to be the American menu for the duration of this internment. For eighty-four days Willi ate canned spinach with the rest of the prisoners, compliments of the American military. In later years, he would heartily remark,

"When I see spinach, then I can throw up! Ask my wife, I think they had spinach stored up in the United States for 50 years!"

Besides the clothes on his back, Willi was half-owner of one blanket. He shared it with a companion who in later years became nameless in Willi's memory. It was odd, and yet not unusual, that some details were remembered vividly and clearly while others were erased, leaving only a smudge to prove that something had occupied that spot. In fact, some prisoners held this "smudgey" look in their eyes even though they looked around, talked, and performed duties; but they reminded

Willi of a toy bird he had as a child. Crudely carved from wood, the legs would move when strings were pulled. To give it life, Willi had taken a piece of charcoal from a cold fire pot and put on some marks to represent eyes and feathers.

"Ya," he thought, as he rubbed his own eyes in an unconscious effort to feel if they were charcoal marks or eyeballs, "some of these guys look like that chicken bird. God Almighty!"

Willi concentrated on the blanket under him so that this wouldn't happen to him. Hours and hours and days and days were spent with that singular shared possession which represented limited warmth and questionable survival, the blanket. That piece of filthy fabric was a fragile tissue between reality and the realm of the unknown. It served as bed, chair, roof, and whatever Willi's imagination and that of his buddy's could make of it.

There was no protection from the elements, until spinach cans became shovels. With empty spinach cans, two men would scoop a hole in the ground like a pair of gophers and over it place a roof of sorts from the cardboard containers in which the spinach had been delivered. Willi and his imprisoned companions lived like this for three months, walking around like animals, with no baths or change of clothing. Because they were always outside, body odor was not a problem. Because they ate spinach, some of them survived.

Then the rains came. It was during this period of time that Willi learned more about how smudges appeared where eyes were supposed to be at Bad Kreuznach. There was a Thief in camp. The rainy, gloomy weather was perfect for his work. This Thief came at all hours, silently, smuggling away pieces of energy and life, the losses of which were registered in the eyes of his victims. Quiet and invisible, he lurked, leech-like, close to the men in the rain. With despair, Willi came to realize that this Thief coveted more than eyes.

The men were sitting around the edge of the infirmary tent that was in the center of the compound. This tent was supposed to represent the merciful assistance of medical aid, but the twenty to twenty-five bodies that came out of it every day gave little encouragement to anyone healthy enough to be watching it. The camp population of 100,000 was dwindling at a steady pace, whether it was hot and sunny or cool and rainy.

On this day the edge of the tent offered some relief from the relentless rain. Willi spent the day there, attempting not to get so wet, while talking. The conversations inevitably turned to mother's cooking, favorite foods, and descriptions of lavish meals eaten in warm kitchens and dining rooms. Details concerning food were always the main topics. During a lull, Willi realized that his neighbor had not spoken for quite a spell. Willi leaned closer and looked. Was he dozing? Was he sick? No, by the merciful Father, he was dead. It was as if in the middle of the conversation, his partner in conversation had departed without saying goodbye. Later in his life, Willi recalled this incident.

"They just fell over like flies. I don't know how to think of it... how to express myself. You could not tell if a guy was sick or anything. He was here and he was gone."

Many men simply slipped away from dehydration or from lack of nutrition. Rather than facing the daily nothingness around them, soldiers who were accustomed to vigorous activity and schedules allowed the Camp Thief to rob them. Silently, each time He came, bringing nothing, He carried away a bit, a slice, a piece of the will to live, until only an exterior remained, like a lamp without its light. And so, on that rainy day, Willi was left speaking to a shell that had been a man.

Willi shivered and thought of returning to his private gopher hole not too far away, but he decided against it. To spend every night down there was enough. The bare dirt was depressing. It matched the feeling in the pit of his stomach. He just sat, rigidly, pretending to be wooden, willing his eyes to look like charcoal colored smears just in case the Camp Thief was still around.

During the next few months, camp time passed slowly for Willi. He tried not to worry about his young Rumanian wife, Lilly, who had been pregnant with their first child when they had been separated by the war. At night it was more difficult to keep a positive attitude. During the day, he was kept busy with assigned jobs in order to keep the camp running. The daily chores kept his mind busy. Many years later he recalled the following events from the warmth and security of a much appreciated home in Bismarck, North Dakota, United States of America.

"This I can say by heart. Nobody can touch me on this. So every day we had to go to work for the American army at Bad Kreuznach. You know, clean kitchen or whatever there was to do. One day we had white people guarding us, taking us to work and one day we had black soldiers guarding us. When white people were guarding us we could never touch any food. They threw away baskets of eggs and bread and butter. So cruel.

"They would throw cigarettes on the ground and when we tried to pick it up they would step on our fingers. This was a sad day when we had the white people. Then came the Negroes. They gave us cigarettes to smoke and went behind the other guards and brought us something to eat because we worked there in the kitchen.

"We called the black soldiers the 'Angels' and the white soldiers the 'Devils' on the same American side. I can tell you this because it was the honest truth. So we were always happy when the second day came and we were guided out by the black people. They knew how we felt, because they were treated the same many years ago.

"Then, in August it came over the loudspeaker,

'Who wants to go home? We need plumbers, carpenters, and electricians. Make yourself ready tomorrow morning.'

"So I signed up as a carpenter. Everybody who signed up was happy. Twelve of us were chosen. Only later did we know that those guys who *didn't* sign up got to go home.

"So, now the ones who signed up are put into open railroad cars. Instead of going in this direction, the train went in the other direction into France. We knew already, now hell starts. Of course, they never told us the truth. Everything was lies from A - Z. Only lies.

"As soon as we passed the French border, the cruelest thing happened. French people poured hot water on us as we went under the over-places... on top of our cars that we were in. That's how cruel. Quite a few of us got burned. I was lucky. I didn't get any. We went to Sedan, northern part of France."

Again Willi observed how the war provided opportunity for those seeking it to inflict unnecessary pain upon other members of the human race.

As Willi rode the train, he reflected. He was thankful for a little luck and a lot of spinach.

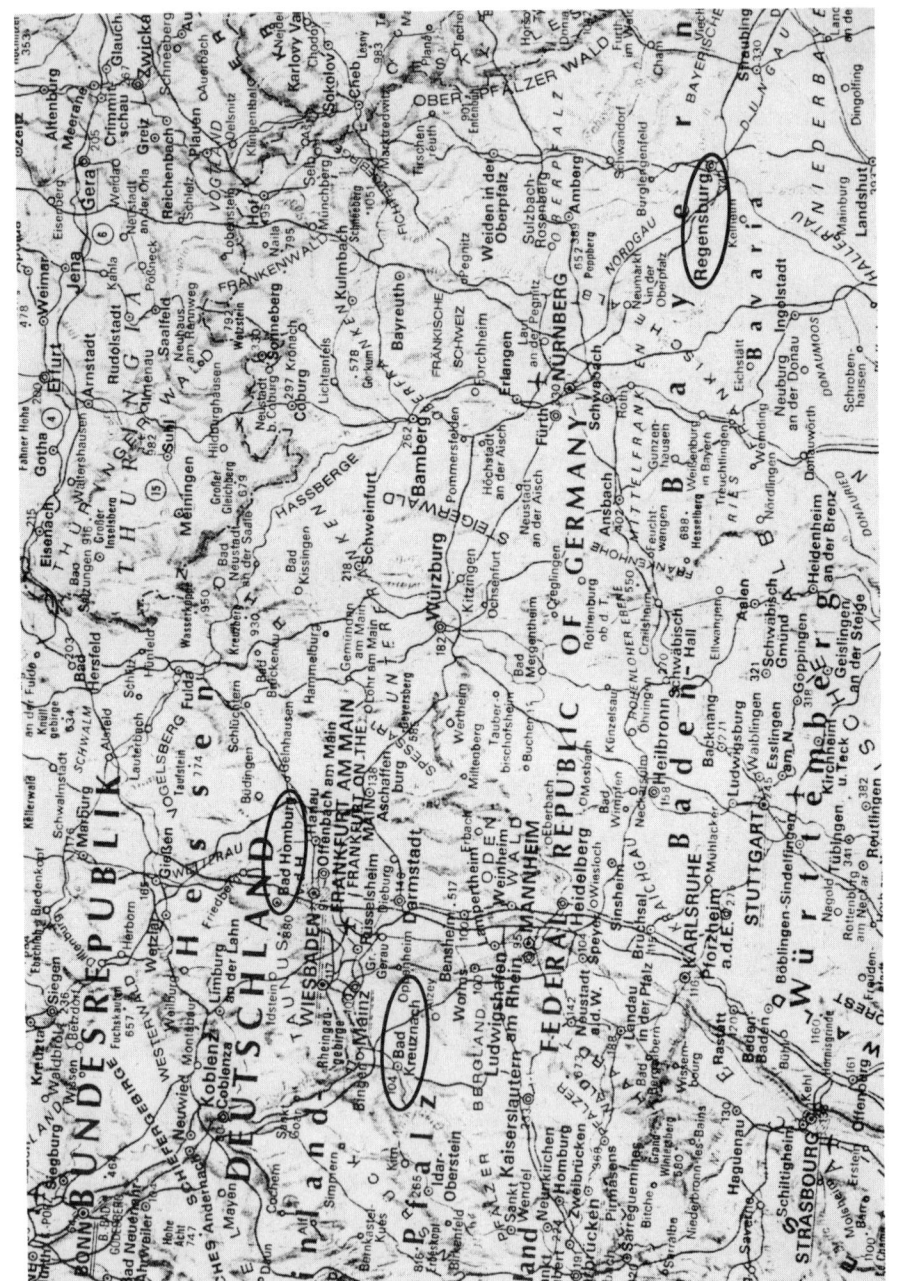

Chapter II
The French Connection

After five years, eight months, and seven days, the European phase of World War II had ended on the Western Front. The cost in lives and money was beyond the comprehension of the average person. Between September of 1939 and September of 1945 more than 10 million Allied servicemen and nearly 6 million military from Axis countries died. The United States alone spent $1,154 billion; not counting property damage.

Willi was not yet aware that Hitler and Mussolini were dead or that the 20th Century treatment of the Jews was to give new meaning to the old Greek term, Holocaust, meaning "whole-burnt," referring to a sacrifice consumed by fire. The systematic rounding up of the Jews and the sophisticated methodology of the killings accomplished the horror of war like never before.

As the Jews were reeling with this enormous cosmic pain, Willi was attempting to deal with his own, which felt cosmic to him. Soviet forces became dominant on the European continent as Sergeant Winger was transported to France. Like a pawn in a political chess game, Willi's life was part of the bargaining between Allies after the war. Decisions were made in February of 1945 at the Yalta Conference by the Big Three, Churchill, Roosevelt, and Stalin. C. L. Sulzberger wrote in *World War II* that these leaders made secret deals in order to wind up the war in Europe and start the rebuilding process. The defeated Reich was divided into four occupied zones and reparations would include the "use of German labor" of which Willi was a part. It was agreed to exchange each other's civilians as they were rounded up in Germany. Willi came to be on his way to Sedan, France, because of these agreements. Some Bad Kreuznach survivors were sold by the Americans to France while others were lucky enough to be sent home during this rebuilding process. Willi was lucky enough to survive, but not lucky enough to go home.

"It was my skills that saved me and also got me into trouble. The farmers went home. I went to France. They wanted electricians, carpenters, like me, or plumbers. People who can do the dirty work. No teachers or medical people. They have enough of them in France."

It was in this French camp that Willi was to meet up with two of his brothers and learn some new lessons. His brother, Oscar, age 21, had been stationed in Italy where the war was well ahead of the Western Front. How he came to be in France at this camp was a mystery to Willi. The other brother, Karl, came from Alsace Lorraine. Under prison circumstances these were not joyous reunions; however, Willi credits Oscar with saving his life. By the time Willi arrived at Sedan, Oscar had been in France for a year as a P.O.W. and Karl showed up two weeks later. To run into both of his brothers here was a small miracle and Willi explained it this way.

"I was at the point where I didn't know either if I ever was going to get out of this or not. What made it so mean was because of our blood type printed under our arms. The SS had it too. I didn't know it at the time. On both my brothers it disappeared, but mine did not disappear. So, they, the French, thought I was SS. They almost killed me."

Willi's interrogation took place in a bare room. As before, there was only a blanket there to help him distinguish reality from the insanity of war conditions.

"They never believed me or my brothers. They, they... they spanked me with their clubs. Three or four guys almost crucified me like Jesus that time. That's how they handled us. Just like tyranny. Not even human. When they were done with me, they put me where the sick people were.

"One night the French doctor came around. He did not know that I speak French and he said to somebody, 'Well, don't worry about that guy, he won't be alive by tomorrow morning.'

"So I thought, 'I going to fool you, you sucker, you know!'

"If not for my brother, I probably wouldn't be here because they would take me to the cemetery from the hospital. I was so weak. My brother Oscar saved my life."

Oscar pleaded, to no avail, with the authorities saying that his brother was not SS. The officers in charge were not convinced. Oscar's own tatoo had faded and also, it was learned later, had Karl's. Different skins reacted differently to the dye.

This incriminating mark took approximately ten years to fade from Willi's skin. The last time he remembered looking at it was in 1952 or 1953. When it was plainly visible in France, three or four men armed with clubs and plenty of hostility did not convince Willi to say anything but the truth about his duties in the German service, which were to interpret, not to investigate.

Oscar was truly his brother's keeper. While Willi lay with multiple bruises and diarrhea from his beatings, Oscar brought bread to him in exchange for Willi's water. Oscar had been working for a farmer and was in comparatively good condition and therefore shared his camp's portion of bread which he smuggled into the hospital under his clothing.

There was no meat or other nutritious food available for camp prisoners in Sedan, but barracks provided protection from the weather. This seemed luxurious to a man who had lived in an open pasture with the elements of nature for months. In Germany it had been water and spinach; in France it was water and bread. Occasionally, a few cabbage leaves floated in the water. This was referred to as soup.

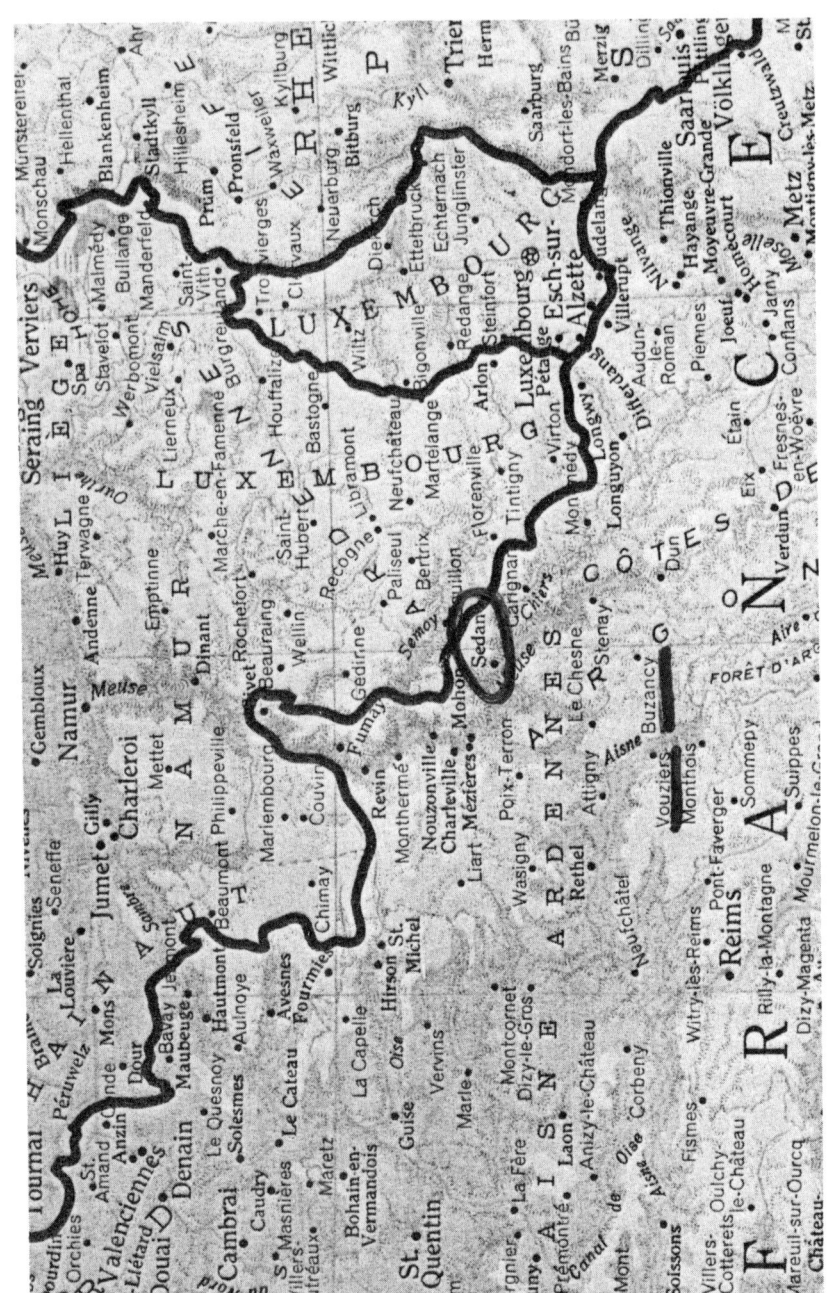

Chapter III
The Forming of the Man

Lying on a hospital cot in Sedan, France, Willi, sick at heart and hurting, knew he was vulnerable. He felt cold. So to warm and protect himself Willi visualized himself as a small speck of burning light that could move about freely. "That's it," he schemed, "I will go back to Rumania, away from here where is all this pain."

To pretend to be mobile was coincidentally appropriate, not only because Willi could psychologically escape his pain and prison environment, but also because he had been born on an Easter Sunday. Set by the ancient Nicene Council, the date varies every year. It is always on the first Sunday after the first full moon on or after March 21 until April 25. Willi's Easter birthdate was March 27, 1921. However, if he wished to celebrate the Easter component of his arrival on the earth, he could move around the calendar a good deal more than other people. He took comfort in that thought.

To pretend to be a speck of light was not unusual either; for in Rumania, Orthodox church goers at Easter Eve would carry lighted candles home. Upon their arrival, they would gaze into a mirror by the light of the candle to see into the future. Yes, his trick was a good one! But he would look to his past instead of the future. He began by thinking of his ancestors.

Willi's grandfather had immigrated to Bessarabia from Stuttgart, Germany, in 1854. Willi's parents, Johannes and Anna Winger were German farmers at Sarata, Bessarabia, where they had been born. Since the day Willi's mother had called his attention to the fact of his Easter birth date, Willi had speculated on the significance of it.

Just what was God's plan for him? Was it God's will or man's that caused him to be in these circumstances?

Rubbing the scar on his face, Willi wondered what added scars and soul wounds he would sustain from this experience. The one on his right cheek had resulted from playing with a dog when he was eight years old. As an adult he had referred to it as his beauty mark, but as a child he remembered how frightened he had been then. "Well, God Almighty, that was nothing compared to this," he thought. Suddenly, he shivered with cold again, and so he actively called up from his depths some warm memories of his youth. He pretended they were printed on cellophane. Pleased with his fantasy, he could unroll them one by one and press them against the windows of his eyes, warding off any possibility of that dreadful smudging that could stifle and steal inner illumination such as he had witnessed at Bad Kreznach. Willi breathed life into his little imaginery point of light in Rumania and recalled the responsibility of being the first born son of nine children. That position of birth in the family had earned him the privilege of learning man's work early in life.

"When I was only seven, I had to ride horses for cultivating like the corn and so. I had to sit the whole day on a horse and drag the plow behind. I had to go out to the fields and work. There was no such thing like sitting around home after school was out."

Large families were needed to work on the family land or in the family business. In the Winger family there were three older sisters, Hilda, Frieda, and Lillie. A second female child had been born after Frieda and had died, in infancy, at approximately age two, due to high fevers and convulsions thought to be caused by teething. Willi was the oldest of four boys—Willi, Oscar, Karl, and Alfred. Marie and Alma were younger sisters.

Thoughts of his father floated into Willi's mind as he recalled how his father had been a proud Russian soldier in World War I. Willi remembered that there had been no arguing with Papa's opinion. He had managed the family with authority and discipline. A wound in the chest from the war had given Willi's father problems. Upon release from his duties as a soldier, he had been x-rayed and informed of shrapnel fragments resting in his chest in an unoperable position. He was instructed to drink large quantities of milk. It was theorized that complications from this wound killed him in 1932 when he was about 42 years old. Willi's mother had believed that slivers from her husband's grenade wound embedded in his chest had split apart and traveled to his heart.

So Willi, just a boy, was put in charge of the Winger family. The lad learned practical problem-solving and assimilated hands-on experience early in life. These skills served him well in later life.

"After my father died, from there on we had a very rough time. We went on with the farming the best we could, but it wasn't the same anymore. When I was thirteen we got up at 2:00 o'clock in the morning. We went out with the hay wagons, loaded them up about ten to twelve feet high, come into town about 8:00 A.M., unloaded, ate, and went back to get some more crop in. Our land was fifteen miles away from town to get the crop in. I was only thirteen and I felt I carried the whole thing myself."

Even though Willi worked hard physically, he preferred to work his mental processes. His sharp mind was captivated by the lure of learning.

"My parents had lots of company at home in Sarata. One time I was in the next room and I heard them talking about me. The way it was down there in Rumania, the oldest son was supposed to take over the family farm or business or whatever. So my father said,

'Forget about Willi. He never going to be a farmer. He gotta' go to school.'

"Of course, when I was a little kid I just wanted to be a teacher. I didn't want to know anything about farming... and so they send me to school and it was very expensive. There was no such thing as scholarships. It was a high price to pay to go to school in Rumania. Because of the war only my youngest brother, Alfred, got to go to college. He was only ten when we went to Germany.

"When I was fourteen years old I entered Verneschule, (Teacher's College). My uncle Otto Winger, from my mother's side, paid for me for three years. My mother's last name was also Winger. Uncle Otto was Catholic. While I did this in the winter, my older sister Hilda did the chores.

"I was a good student. I never had girl friends when I had my books. Girl friends didn't mean nothing to me. My books were the most important thing. Of course, I had friends. The young people, teenagers, in a group always wanted to be tougher than others and then they got in fights. I never went along with anything like this. Whenever there was something going on like this, I left. I never engaged in any beating up or arguing on the streets. I always disappeared. It was against my nature.

"I decided to be a cabinet maker. So I went two years to school for this. We had to pay to learn. When I was approximately eighteen or so, I made my license to become a cabinet maker. It was 1939. I worked on my own for one year in Sarata and then the Russians came and we ran to Germany."

It was evident early in Willi's life that as well as being a good worker, he was a good thinker and communicator. Some of this resulted from the schooling he had, of course, but other aspects of his surroundings encouraged this part of his personality.

One of these was the family and community emphasis put on religion. Guidelines were established early for treating others fairly and for "trusting in the Lord" to bring events into an optimistic point of view. Willi's father and mother insisted on consistent church attendance and Willi's grandmother, his father's mother, and her son, who was a pastor, were personal role models for Christian standards. It was also their influence that led to his interest in playing the organ.

"It was right away my first grade teacher who showed me the notes on the organ. And, of course, my uncle was a pastor and he helped me along. Since my grandmother was so old, she couldn't go to church anymore. My uncle would come there to give her communion and I always played the organ. That's how I started.

"My best memory when I was eight or a little more was when I go to my aunt's, that was married to the pastor, with presents to exchange with my cousins for Christmas. A poor man had come to my uncle the day before and asked for a shirt because he wanted to go to church on Christmas. So my uncle gave him his best shirt, so when I got there that day, my aunt was mad. He gave up his best shirt to that poor man, but my aunt was mad like everything! I never forgot that in my life yet! My uncle said to me,

'Remember all your life, it is so much nicer to give than to receive.'

"This stays in my mind today yet and what I still like to do whenever I get a chance."

Being surrounded by extended family in those early days was comforting to reflect on while in the prison hospital at Sedan. Willi tried to find a more comfortable position for his battered body. As he shifted and felt a flash of pain, he suddenly remembered another beating he had survived. That one he could smile about. It was, however, a vivid lesson.

"On my 16th birthday, we were four friends together. We had them black sheeps. They were curly hairs. They were very, very expensive lambs. One lamb brought more in than a big cow. My friend was living only a few houses from us. One particular day he had born two of them little lambs.

"I had on my very first beautiful black suit and it was on a Sunday. We were looking at them lambs and one crazy guy came up with the idea ... 'Oh, we got to celebrate!'

"There was a big restaurant at the train depot with a bar and we went in there and we drink wine till it came over the top! On the way home we needed the whole street. At that time there was no cars or nothing, so you didn't have to worry. So, I came home and I felt terrible. I went to the shed where we had hay stacked and I lay me in the stack with my new suit.

"My sister Lillie seen me go in there. So she came with a great, big broom and she spanked me until everything was gone out! So I was sober again. Then I had to change my suit and go to work. It was the very first time I was drunk."

Willi had the soothing ability to forgive his sister for his switching and to forgive himself for drinking too much. This approach to problems became his trademark later in life. It was a manner of detachment, an attitude of accepting reality at face value while incorporating an expansive and comforting concept of forgiveness. Thinking of his beating, Willi speculated that his sister Lilly probably had done him a favor in the way of preparation. Also, he realized his family's religious expectations had guided him. Somehow, he knew that all of these lessons had something to do with his relationship to God.

"We were raised very religious, Evangelical Lutherans. As soon as the sun went down on Saturday evening, nobody touched nothing anymore. Everything had to be spic and span; the whole yard had to be clean. Of course, we had to feed our animals, but that was the only thing. Sunday School and Confirmation were only natural. On Sunday there was really no big meal. For example, my mother made milk soup or wine soup... something like cream of wheat. Nothing that was lots of work.

"There was no mixing of religious people around Sarata. One town in the whole province of Bessarabia was Catholic, I think... that was Paris, completely by themselves. Across the Dnieper River there were more Catholics than Lutherans."

Although religious impressions were provincial, cultural persuasions were pluralistic. The area near the Black Sea where Willi spent his childhood was inhabited by Russian, Bulgarian, Muldavian, and many German people, including the Cachuptas and the Gypsies. Many languages and dialects were spoken. The Rumanian culture and language were intertwined delicately. Willi's own family spoke Schwabish German. His ears and brain at a young age became accustomed to the sound of many tongues and he learned early to accept behaviors and beliefs of other traditions than his own. His warm-hearted disposition could not be ignored by those around him. He attributed much of this to the Russian people who surrounded him when he was small.

"Before Communism, the Russian people were one of the most religious people. They gave more than anyone else. They were the most warm-hearted, if they were not Communist. The Russian people would give his last shirt or his last pants so you got something to wear.

"For example, like summertimes, we had up to ten or fifteen Russian peoples working for us when my father was alive. We had great big goings on on our farm. You could not find any better people for work or entertainment. Actually, Russian people raised us kids. Our mother and father didn't have time for us. They hired Russians. We had one guy who lived with us all year long, a permanent worker. You could not find a better people. They lived only ten miles from Sarata, a complete Russian settlement called Plachtievka."

Some of the "goings on" that Willi remembered were the activities scheduled around the grape growing season. Many of the farmers made their own wine and some of them had commercial operations. The Winger wine press was only six feet in diameter, a small operation. However, all available hands were needed, so naturally, the children were put to work.

"Nine kids had to go pick grapes. It was a holiday to us until the stomach was full. Then it was no more fun. A memorable thing was there was lots of watermelon and grapes. And we would just have a break and eat bread, butter, watermelon, grapes, or cantaloupes.

"Then Mother went in the evening to milking cows. So everybody had a cup. We did not have supper in the summertime. We were right there standing with our cup and that was that. It was finished. She didn't have to make any supper.

"Later, if you would drink milk from the cow they say you'll be dead tomorrow. That's not practical, that you can not drink milk without going through processing. And nobody was sick. We were all healthy, every single one of us."*

Suddenly, Willi's thoughts about milk were interrupted by the reality of his deprivation. Staring at the dirty ceiling of the Sedan hospital, he wet his lips. His mouth and stomach were longing for a cup of milk. It was some time before his taste buds would cooperate well enough in order to resume active dreams of home.

Times had been good growing up as a farm boy in Rumania, even though the government was in turmoil. After World War I the Rumanian people demanded more liberal land reforms. This was granted by a democratic and more liberal constitution in 1923; however, the worldwide depression of 1929 brought severe hardship once again. Both Willi and his wife were born into these sparse economic years, but there had always been food, shelter, and a secure family network with which to share.

During the restless years between World War I and World War II, King Carol wished for Rumania to stay

---

*Johann David Idler related some parallel experiences to Willi's in an article entitled "Memories of Johann David Idler From Sarata, Bessarabia," included in the Journal of American Historical Society of Germans from Russia, Vol. 11, No. 4, Winter 1988, with pictures.

neutral, but he was forced to surrender land when Italy entered the war. Russia demanded Bessarabia and northern Bucovina. Both Willi's family and his wife's were moved about like refuse before the mechanical motions of the World War II machine. Their lives would be forever affected by the evacuation of Rumanian civilians from their homes to many camps in Germany in order to avoid the powerful Russians. Hitler had sold them out.

Hitler and Stalin became allies and signed a nonagression pact on August 23, 1939. They agreed not to go against each other; they wanted to divide Poland between themselves. Hitler granted Moscow permission to take Bessarabia from Rumania and in return Stalin promised to supply Germany with raw materials and help suppress the Poles.

When King Carol was forced to abdicate in September of 1940, his son Michael became a king with no power. The country of Rumania was ruled by General Ion Antonescru, who was appointed premier on September 4, 1940. Antonescru worked closely with the Germans who occupied Rumania at that time, but the relationship was an uneasy one. Eventually, the Rumanians gained back the land of Bessarabia from the Russians by their alliance with Germany, but not before many citizens were uprooted and families torn apart. In early 1940 Russia traded wheat to Germany for the properties left in Bessarabia by Rumanians fleeing to Germany. This trade was just one small decision in Hitler's dream to conquer the world. This upheaval came just as young Willi was engaged in sharpening his skills as a cabinet maker.

Willi's family packed up and left Sarata. Their destination was Galatz where all refugees would board a ship to travel up the Danube River. Willi stayed behind to help others load up. At approximately age 19, he arrived at a holding camp at Schlukenau (Sluknov), Czechoslovakia, and from there was drafted into the German infantry. Five years later his journey had brought him here to Sedan, France.

In 1921, among the hayfields of Rumania, on an Easter Sunday, a pin-prick of light began to glow—just another twentieth century glimmer, among millions. Fueled with the energy of youth and pushed by the powerful Communist and Nazi winds that swept out of the north and across Europe, the tiny ember moved . . . to Czechoslovakia, then to Germany, appearing briefly in Poland, glowing in Russia, shining again in Germany, and now barely flickering in France.

Willi cleared his throat and the sound brought him back to reality. He was half-dead, except for a very alive imagination, longing for a cup of fresh milk.

Willi Winger as a young German soldier, October of 1941, with his sister Frieda and her family.

Willi's family: Standing from left Willi, Alfred, Frieda, Mother, Oscar, Lillie, Hilda, Alma, Karl, Marie—1959.

Chapter IV
The Not So Great Escape

Somehow, probably through the other prisoners, authorities at Sedan discovered that the man they had nearly beaten to death was the only German prisoner in camp who could speak French. After Willi recovered, thanks to Oscar, the French commanded Willi's services to interpret for them. Willy was dismayed, but, of course, there was no alternative.

"After they killed me almost, then whenever they needed somebody, they called me as an interpreter. So then I could not say we were mistreated at Bad Kreuznach by the Americans, except for the lack of food and water. The French fixed me worse."

When Willi recuperated enough to leave the hospital quarters, he mingled with the others and during this time found to his surprise another coincidence. A fellow prisoner with whom he visited turned out to be a relative to Lilly, his new wife. This man had grown up in the same general area as Willi and Lilly.

"Then the guy disappeared. And, of course, something like this, you don't dare look for an answer or anything what happened. I thought maybe he died or whatever."

Willi was more disheartened by the fact that this comrade had no news of Lilly's welfare than he was by the fact that the fellow disappeared. Willi wondered if he were getting so acclimated to camp living, so calloused, that nothing could shock him any longer. But he knew he was sick to death of it and wanted to see his loved ones. Sharing these thoughts with others, Willi and fellow captives decided it was time to be aggressive. They attempted to flee the French.

"Oscar and me and two more guys, on a very, very dark night, tried to escape. We went through the wires. For some reason we lost each other in the dark. Two of us got away and two got caught. We were out almost all night. We were a very short time from the Belgium border. If we probably could have went another two hours, we would be safe like the other ones. I was one that got caught. Oscar made it out.

"Camp guards knew we were missing. They sent out patrols. There was nothing we could do. They just took us back. You could not do any resistance. No, you dare don't fight. They would shoot you down.

"I didn't see Oscar for two and a half years and the other two guys I never saw again. The camp disappeared, but while I was there I didn't have the energy to try to escape again."

Optimism was restored again, however, by the arrival of a letter from Lilly. It informed him that she was alive and well and that Willi was the father of a baby boy! Lilly's cousin had been released from Sedan and had relayed the location of Willi's imprisonment to Willi's family. Willi read the letter over and over again. The psychological reality of war was compounded by the fact that politcally it was finished while his suffering continued; but now he knew he would make it. He said a final farewell to his depression. Reading that letter was like feeling the Rumanian sun shining on his back . . . and now, that warm, yellow shawl which had draped about his shoulders and neck while in the fields of his boyhood engulfed his heart and comforted him so that he knew his spirit would shine another day.

Chapter V
Slave Labor

The political chess game continued as the French government moved prisoners like pawns. Arrangements were made to put men to work outside of the camp for neighboring citizens who paid money for these services to the French government. Willi compared it to a slave market.

"I was there two months in Sedan when I heard the loudspeaker talk for so many carpenters, plumbers, electicians etc. So, again I give my resume. Here is hell, anyway, so maybe it will be better.

"So we were twelve people who signed up. Here comes a heavy, husky guy . . . a 'Sgt. Schultz' type. I hope I never get to this guy or I might see more hell than I ever did before! He looked us over. He asked for somebody what speaks French. They point to me. I wanted to die. Now I really going to have it! I couldn't do nothing. He picked me, so I have to go.

"So let's go. It was about noon time and that guy took me in his car. The first thing that guy did, he took me to a very beautiful restaurant and gave me to eat, so that I could hardly walk anymore! Then we drove from Sedan, south to Buzancy, a small town like a county seat. By now, it was late afternoon and he took me to another place to eat and I think this is started out pretty darn good!

"I wish I could remember the guy's name yet. Then we went to his home at a small town named Vouziers in the Bucancy (Buzancy) county. He had a son exactly my age who was a cabinet maker too. He had a wife and there were three or four other people there too.

"The first two weeks they watched me very, very close. Then they found out they didn't have to tell me anything. You make this and this, and it was made! I was much more a cabinet maker than his son or the whole crew. Finally, he said,

'How about if I send you out? You go with my son.'

"And I like it. I could speak the French nice. It came to the point where the people like me there. I was happy to be with other people to talk, the whole town really. I lived in their home and I was not guarded anymore or anything. But they made sure if I tried to escape they would be right on my butt. I had to sign a paper to get out of camp that I would work there a whole year.

"This man had to pay the French government for every hour I worked. I can not tell you exactly anymore, but the year and one-half I worked there I earned enough to buy me one suit. Everything else went to the government. It was like a slave market.

"I was lucky to find a man that understood I was not a criminal. I was a good worker. I never talked back. What they said to do I done and they really appreciated it. Of course, I slept in a room next to theirs, so there was no way I could get lost in the night. His wife was always so kind and sweet. She never let me know any anger. She didn't treat me like a prisoner. She treated me as a human, very nice.

"People know already just by talking to me that I like to talk a little bit and these folks enjoyed that. I always had a humor. I was not hanging my face down. That made a good impression on them.

"Other people in Vouziers understood that I was not a criminal. I did only my duty like any other soldier because I had no other chance. And they finally realized there was nothing wrong and like I say, all the way through, they enjoyed having me there."

Willi's charming delight in something about himself and in others was an asset through the war years and it would prove as well to be in future years. This same attribute served him well in his communication duties as a clerk and an interpreter. Underlying his obvious good will, however, there rested a feeling of iron and a certain aloofness. His ability to disengage psychologically when he wished provided strength many times for a German youth caught up in an active military age. It kept the Camp Thief out at Bad Kreuznach; it harbored his warm heart through the beatings at Sedan; it helped him to talk and laugh and live when he wanted to scream and cry and die. In later years, he could easily slip into his mode of detachment when recalling hardships that he and his family suffered in order to speak calmly about them. The natural inner light, warming this iron personality, was consciously kindled by his instinct for survival and his struggle for dignity amidst the chaos of prison circumstances. It was this partnership of good will and iron will that governed the way Willi treated others and consequently, the way others treated him as his life progressed. He perceived his personality as being quite popular with the French.

"Then passed by about three weeks since I came to their home. So Sunday morning came and my French boss questions,

'How about going with us to church?'

"And, of course, in France everything is French Catholic, you know. There's no such thing like the Lutherans. I said,

'Why not? There's nothing else to do anyhow.'

"So I went with them people to church in Vouziers and the priest there for some reason in two minutes, right away, he had his eyes on me. I don't know what he thought of, what's coming here or what's going on, whatever, anyhow, after we shook hands, he said,

'I hope you come back next Sunday too again.'

"I never knew even what means Catholic. I never was in a Catholic church before in my life and I really started to enjoying it. So I went every Sunday."

After one particular service, the priest came by and said to Willi,

33

"How about it? Can I make a Catholic out of you?"
With a laugh Willi replied,
"Maybe when I am a free man I will think about it!"
Willi thought that being with Catholic Christians sure was better than sitting in his room all alone. It gave him security to go to these Catholic services. That priest probably wouldn't want him anyway if he knew that right at that moment Willi's Lutheran soul was more interested in what had happened to Lilly than in what might happen in a Catholic church.

Chapter VI
Lilly

On Sundays after church when Willi had time to rest from his duties in France, he reminisced with reverential regard about the love of his life. As a child in Sarata, he had no way of knowing that his life-time mate was growing up not far from his home territory.

Born under the sign of Leo, August 20, 1920, a sandy-haired female child entered the lives of Nathaniel and Clara Mayer. Indeed, her sign was prophetic as she faced the events of a life interrupted by a war with the skill and courage of a warm-hearted lioness. She was reared in a place named Schabo, Rumania, south of Odessa and east of Sarata. This daughter, christened Lilly, joined an older brother, Leo. Both of them attended country school and then went into Belze for high school education. Lilly viewed Leo as an added father figure in her life since he was eight years older than she.

"My brother Leo liked to take me fishing always and I didn't like it. I said,

'I can not fish!'

"He said, 'You can do everything, but you can not take a step ladder to go up to heaven.'

"Well, I still don't like fishing!"

As in Willi's environment, Lilly also had a multitude of hired people around and much activity stimulating her early years. The family had Arabian horses used for breeding and large wine presses which were operated by hand. Many workers were required to help handle the horses and the vineyards during the grape producing season.

Willi remembered that his wife always spoke happily about the horses. He could hear her voice now, as if she were seated next to him in this room. She was saying,

"I had a horse I liked then named Lady. My father always had horses and he would sell them. My father was very good to horses. They followed him, especially the foals. He had always in his pocket the sugar and he talked to them.

'Up, up,' he said, So they came up and put their front feet here, you know."

Willi envisioned Lilly touching her chest and shoulders to demonstrate as she told her story to their friends.

"And they put their noses in his pocket to get the sugar out.

"I had an uncle, Uncle Willy. He raised horses too and he went every year to Bucharest to the horse races. The horses were a pride for the man, you know. They had a saying down there; I think it is the most cruel thing.

'Weibersterben macht dem Bauer kein Verderben,
aber Pferdeverrecken das macht Schrecken.'*
(When a woman dies, it is unfortunate,
But when a horse dies, it is a tragedy.)"

Willi crossed and uncrossed his legs. The wooden chair on which he was seated in order to gaze out the window of his room in France was uncomfortable, or was it that severe look, even though only recollected, that Lilly had directed at him when telling about that old saying that made him fidget? He could feel her eyes sending signals from the past. She always sparked up when she talked about her family or memories from her childhood.

"My father used to take me along always to pick the grapes and other fruits. We had all kinds of fruits, apricots, pears. One time it was so funny. You know when we press

---

*Standard High German: Several variations of this old German-Russian saying exists. See Shirley Fischer Arends' *The Central Dakota Germans: Their History, Language, and Culture,* page 148; pub. by Georgetown University Press.

out the grapes, the stuff that was left, we throw it out to the pigs to eat; and of course, they don't eat it right away and it started fermenting. I had my pet pig. At that time I was small and I was riding all over on his back, you know.

"Uuuuggh, uuuuggh, finally he had enough with me and then he sat down and I slid down and I was mad. I hit him and hit him, but he didn't go. He was too drunk!"

She would laugh vivaciously, enjoying her own joke, and Willi would too, never tiring of it, he remembered.

The wine and grapes, along with other produce that was grown in that southern soil and climate were taken down to the wharf to be picked up by ships. These wares were carried in barrels, bottles, and baskets and transported to port by wagons. Lilly's young mind was forever influenced by a particular incident that she witnessed while at the docks one day with her father. It involved the home-brewed alcohol of the area.

Some sailors and fishermen were drinking vodka and also smoking. After lighting his cigarette, a man threw away his match carelessly close to another man drinking vodka. The match ignited the brew near the drinking man's mouth and it burned him so severely he died. The vodka was 100% alcohol. Willi knew that Lilly's timid approach to the use of alcohol stemmed from this incident.

Rumanian folklore fascinated Lilly. She loved to repeat the many picturesque stories about the gypsies and share her own experiences with them. The mellow climate allowed the nomads to live comfortably in their wagons most of the year. Some believed they had special powers or healing magic. Willi remembered their coming to his family's place, also. When he was 16 years old the gypsies convinced him that urinating on a wart under a full moon would shrink it. He sighed, as he thought of those innocent and naive days. He liked the story Lilly told about her father's toothache.

"My father had a lot of customers. He sold wine and grapes. There were always many people. One day he had a toothache. Some gypsy came by and she saw him hold his cheek and she said,

'Boss, are you having a toothache?'

'Ya, I have toothache.'

'Come with me!'

"First he didn't want to go. So, she took him by the sleeve around the building. She was talking something and taking soil from the ground and putting it on his face and talking again. Then she said,

'Now you can go back to your work.'

"Then when he was talking to the customers, he realized his toothache was gone."

Lilly's attitude was very tolerant of these Rumanian roamers.

"They have some kind of power, those gypsies. They would steal your chickens, if they get a chance. Right from the stall in Bessarabia. Five to seven wagons would come by with a dozen kids. One kid would be here and one there. There was nothing you could do about it. Everytime you turn around there was something missing. They didn't harm you. They needed food. Then they sold things they stole from the other guy down the road."

Not all events were this mellow in Lilly's childhood. A gigantic "hammer-and-sickle" shadow was cast over the Mayer family and their property when Lilly was eight years old, in 1928. Nathaniel Mayer owned land across the Dnieper River in Russia where he had wineries. He received papers from the Communist government that he was soon to be transported to Siberia because of unpaid taxes on the land within the Russian border. Word spread quickly throughout the Schabo area about Nathaniel's bad luck. The night before the Communist authorities were to arrest Nathaniel, a Russian peasant, who had worked for Nathaniel since he was a boy, came to the Mayer household to offer help.

When this worker had matured and married, Nathaniel had given, as a wedding present, some land, a wagon, and two oxen. Now, wishing to repay Nathaniel's generosity, the Russian man proposed passage to Bulgaria on a friend's fishing vessel in order to avoid deportation to Siberia. Immediately, bare necessities were loaded into a wagon which took the four Mayers and their loyal worker to the Black Sea coast. There the family boarded a fishing boat and headed south to Bulgaria where they would be safe.

The occupants of the boat froze in fear when out of the darkness a water patrol signaled to stop. Wishing to protect his passengers, the Russian fisherman signaled a reply in return that he was on a fishing run. The group was frozen in terror waiting for a return signal, or worse, a gesture that they would be boarded. After some inspection from a distance the patrol crew allowed the fishing boat to continue. When the Mayers disembarked later, Nathaniel made an agreement with the fisherman. In case the authorities were to arrest him on the return voyage, a letter should be posted saying that he (the fisherman) was in the hospital. This way the Mayers would know of his welfare after they parted.

To the dismay of the Mayers, a letter arrived shortly from the fisherman reporting that he was indeed in the hospital and was quite sick. This news was very depressing to the family, but they could do nothing.

While in Bulgaria, Leo and his father found work in a greenhouse. The family survived on fruit. In two months time the Bulgarian government allowed Nathaniel to write home to Schabo for his papers so that he could be allowed to return to Schabo with his family by train.

In the absence of the Mayer family, renters and a sister of Lilly's mother had maintained the farm somewhat; however, the fruit crop was grossly neglected. The family was so thankful to return safely that the withered vines and other damage seemed small problems to solve. It was never discovered what had happened to the brave fisherman.

In spite of these problems, Lilly's parents, Nathaniel and Clara Mayer, had provided an extremely comfortable childhood for their family in Schabo, approximately 45 kilometers southeast of Sarata. Little did the family realize that a larger and darker shadow than the Communist tax problem was creeping upon them. The luxury of a stable, secure home disappeared on September 24, 1940, when the family packed up everything they could and headed for Galatz. Lilly was twenty years old when Moscow took Bessarabia from Rumania.

The Mayers left Schabo and went by horses and wagon to Sarata where they collected other relatives. Nathaniel Mayer was a wagonmaster, so Clara helped to see that horses received proper oats and hay. Clara was a nature-loving person and took these traveling duties in stride with a calm and gentle attitude.

Just as in Willi's case, the younger men from Schabo were left behind to assist those who had no wagons or to see that everybody got out. Women, children, and older men went ahead. The trip to the port of Galatz on the Danube River was a sad one, because of the separation from land, home, and memories; however, much worse was in store when, upon their arrival, all possessions were confiscated by the Russian authorities. Later, after Willi and Lilly had talked about it with others, Willi could remember how his wife's voice clouded with emotion.

Willi jerked his head up. His thoughts were so vivid he was sure that his French friends could hear them in their parlor. Images of Lilly at the mercy of the Russians were not pleasant. Surrounded by nourishing food and work here in France, Willi's strength and confidence had returned. He suddenly was overwhelmed with visions of Lilly being denied the comforts they had both enjoyed before the curse of war had interfered. He was hungry for more news of his wife and son. What was happening to them in this hell-hole of a war and its aftermath?

He lowered his eyes, folded his arms across his chest, and returned to the Rumanian border in his mind where he heard Lilly speaking...

"When Hitler made agreement with the Russians to take all the Germans out, they say we can not have more than one wedding ring and one watch. Some people made holes in the wagon tongues and stuck in a watch or rings or whatever, but the Russians found everything. They said what you can do is put everything in one envelope and we give it to the Germans and they would put our name on and give it back. But to this day we got nothing. The Russian Communists took everything, but never gave a thing back.

"I take a chance, but by the border they come with some kind of little machine (a geiger counter) that goes tick, tick, tick, and finds everything. In other words, from the time we left the house there was lies, lies, lies until we got to Bismarck in the United States of America. Every time they told us something, they lied, everybody. We were there with nothing."

Willi actively resisted the depressive mood that accompanied these thoughts. He knew Lilly's trip had been like his and their other relatives and friends. In his mind, she continued,

"Then in October the men that were left back home had to tie up whatever they could on horses. The swindle started again. They could drive up to the ship; then the horses were taken away. They were left standing with their empty hands. The Communists let us have everything until we got to the ship and they they took everything away except maybe a pack of cigarettes. No money, no nothing, absolutely nothing! That's what made people so sick and angry. My beautiful horses and everything was gone!"

The Mayer family spent approximately a year in a refugee camp at Rumberg, Czeckoslovakia. It was here that their papers were examined and their arms tattooed with blood types. Then later they were sent with many others from Bessarabia to Poland to farm at Niederland where they were assigned the correct amount of land, according to what they had owned in Rumania. Lilly and her parents were located close to Jarocin where Lilly took Red Cross training and her family farmed and had horses again. Brother Leo was not with them. He had volunteered for the German army when he was about 26 years old. Willi had last seen his bride of six months there in Poland.

During this refugee period Willi had been placed in a holding camp at Schluckenau, close to Rumberg, where he was put to work making furniture. Frieda was married and with her husband, but Willi's mother, sister Lillie, and his three brothers were there also. Hilda went to Wiesbaden directly from the ship. The Winger family was transferred to Prosnadorf, Poland, where land was parceled out to them by the German government in the same manner as with the Mayers.

Suddenly, the sound of supper call brought Willi back from Poland to the room in France that held him prisoner. His Rumanian travelogue was at an end. He had arranged a meeting of the minds with Lilly. It was the best he could do for now.

Lilly with her parents, Nathanial and Clara Mayer.

The Meyers with children, Lilly and Leo.

CZECHOSLAVIA

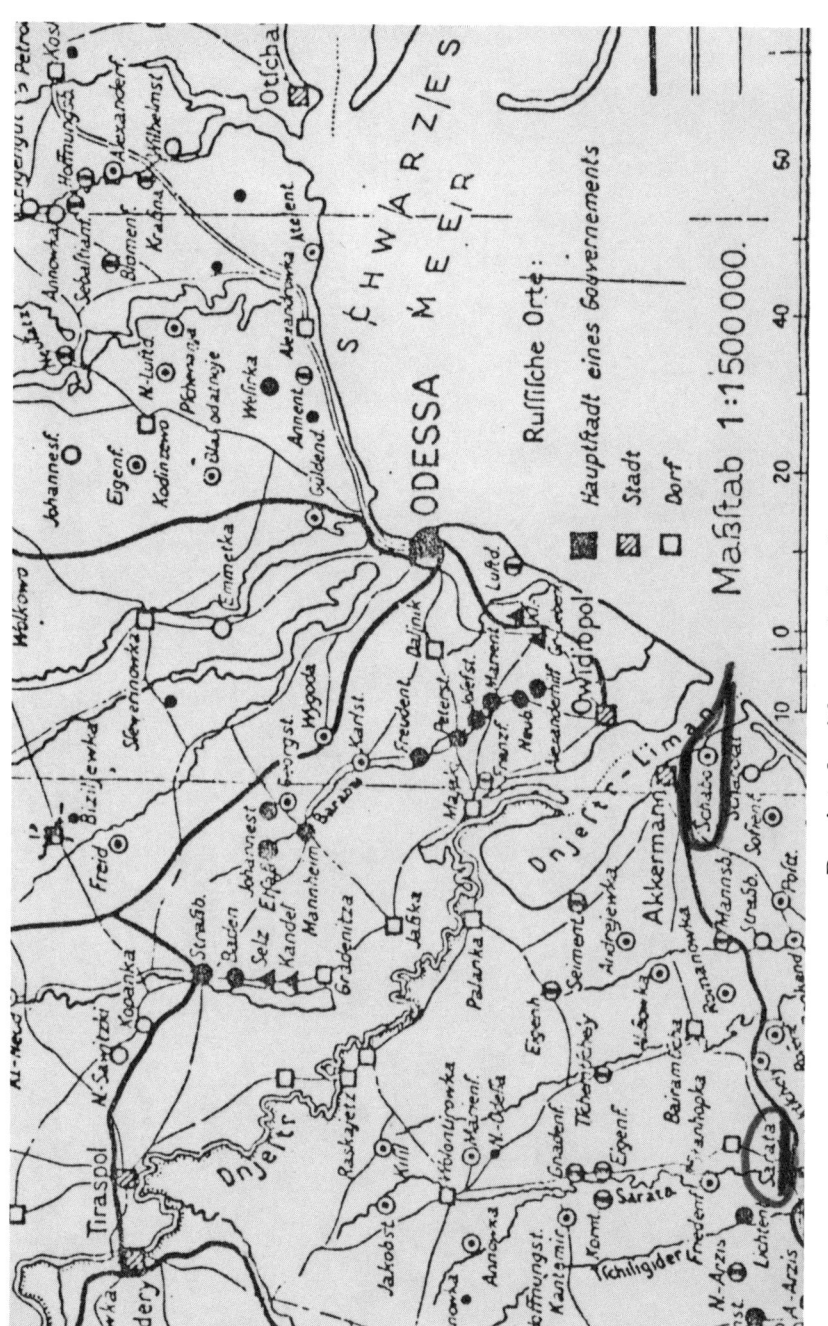

Reprinted with permission from
The Bertsch Book—222 Years by Harry A. Delker

Chapter VII
Leaving Bessarabia

Willi had a Sunday meal with his post-war warden and family and then spent the rest of the evening mulling in his room. It was his only diversion. He returned to thoughts of 1939 and 1940.

Leaving Bessarabia had been an adventure for Willi and his young buddies. With youthful optimism there was little of the pain of separation and less anxiety for the future than for the older generation who were forced to leave their life's work behind.

The political upheaval in Europe was reflected vividly in the fleeing families. Women and children were wrenched from husbands and fathers, living in separate quarters or camps. Properties were lost and relationships were changed forever. Later in life Willi and Lilly recalled that sometimes fathers and grandfathers had wept before their stunned families when horses and wagons were confiscated. Other families had wept communally. Willi remembered older people in Sudedengau camp nearby that found the situation just too difficult to absorb.

"That was very tragic. For the young, who cares? Now the elderly people, 50 or 60, there were many suicides because they could not bring it over their hearts to lose everything and just stay with nothing. In Rumania our families were rich people and now we are the poorest in the world. They could not take it. To be rich and then completely poor. They just hanged themselves.

"Our own neighbor did it in Germany. At home there was no poor German. The poor people in Sarata were the Russians and Bulgarians that worked for us. After my father passed away and even when my mother could not afford my expensive school, we had our land, cows, horses, and everything."

Willi thought about his own mother who had been depressed by camp living. She had so much time on her hands while the others were working at various jobs. At the time Willi and many of his young counterparts didn't realize or hardly cared that most of them would never see Bessarabia again. This exodus was one that would be remembered, not only by the exiles, but by those who viewed it and indirectly were influenced by it in later generations. The Winger and Mayer families represented a microcosm of the whole as they left their homeland of Bessarabia.

Chapter VIII
Willi Winger and Lilly Mayer Meet
BUND

Lilly was initially introduced to the Winger family in Sarata where she attended meetings of the Bunt Deutscher Mädel, an organization developed for the females of Hitler's youth. Marie Winger was also among its members.

So by the time the Mayer family gathered relatives in Sarata, traveled to the port of Galatz, and were evacuated to Czechoslovakia, Lilly was best friends with Marie Winger and was fairly well acquainted with other members of the family. The mass of Bessarabien refugees was a congregation of extended families and neighbors clumped together like the grapes they cut from the vine with a scissors in the fall, placed in baskets, transferred to barrels, and transported to unknown markets. It turned out that the two families, Wingers and Mayers, would be neighbors in refugee camps somewhat similiar to their locations in Bessarabia. In this uncertain and restricted setting, a young Rumanian woodworker from Sarata and a vibrant girl from the vineyards of Schabo began a wartime romance.

Willi and Lilly were formally introduced at a camp dance in Schluckenau by Herbert Miller, a friend of Willi's who had been courting Lilly. Camp dances were enjoyed by the young people. They made the best of their temporary, transient time of life by doing the polka, waltz, and slow tango. Soon after his introduction to Lilly and wishing to explore the relationship further, Willi made plans to travel the ten miles to the Rumberg camp where Lilly lived with her parents.

"We were in Schluckenau and they were in Rumberg. We had met in Schluckenau. So the next Saturday, I said to myself I'm going to come to Rumberg where she was. So I got on the train. I stepped out and I went to the camp and there I was waiting for Fraulein Mayer. There comes a lady along with Lilly with a big, big hat just like them Mexican things!"

A short, hardly audible chuckle escaped Willi's throat as he reflected. He remembered Lilly's objections to his teasing about her mother's hat.

"No, that's not true. You just disappeared around the corner. Then we had coffee together. Momma came out with me and you saw her and got scared, you schtinker!"

Willi had continued his playfulness and had put on a mask of fake fear and countered,

"With that big straw hat, I got scared and left. That's how shy I was, you know."

Lilly had dismissed his attempt at humor with a wave of her hand and defended her beloved Mama.

"She always dressed nice. Everytime Papa had a good sale, he bought her a dress and matching shoes and jewelry. I remember a nice lily of the valley brooch with all pearls, real pearls. It was beautiful."

In reflection, those things didn't mean much now after all that they had been through. Willi just wished he could see their faces again, which were like jewels to him.

As a young refugee, Lilly spent considerable time in the camps with family and neighbors. The young people found diversions to entertain themselves during those nomadic times of the early 1940's.

"Rumberg was pretty nice. Even though we were allowed only our clothes, one watch and one ring, we had school and good food. The buildings, like empty schools, were fixed for us and they put in beds, like a barracks. My folks could be with me there.

"And we had fun playing tricks on the boys. The mattresses were filled with straw. So when the boys were out, we cut them open and put in blocks of wood and sewed the mattress together again ... or sometimes we put in water. And when they came home late at night, we could hear them screaming and hollering upstairs. We played all kinds of tricks on them.

"The German government put me to work doing typing and bookwork. I had the goal to be a Home Economics teacher and went to Wiesbaden, but on vacation got papers for the Red Cross instead.

"Then we were drafted too, just like the soldiers, young women. We were put to work in a factory where they made over corn leaves into camouflage to cover up the ammunitions. The leaves were dyed green and put into a machine that looked like all wires. It was made to look like a blanket. They drafted me in this. But then we were sent to Niederland in Poland.

"I took my training for Red Cross in Jarocin, a town where the train came through with the wounded soldiers from the Russian front. We dressed the wounds and gave them first aid, fed them, washed then, clothed them, and they were shipped to the hospital. We didn't have much. It was war. We gave them what we could ... just first aid. We had one or two doctors for the whole thing.

"We also had two trains coming in with Germans from Russia, not Bessarabia or Rumania, from the Ukraine. They were fleeing from the Communists, like we had. Usually there were no men. See, when the bombs came down and the mother was killed and the child was left, that's when they came to Jarocin. We fed them and cleaned them up too."

Getting to work on a bicycle was sometimes perilous. On one occasion Lilly was stopped by two Polish partisans with guns. They recognized her Red Cross uniform as a German one and demanded identification. She shook in fright when they jerked her bodily from her bicycle and argued in Polish. When they released her she was shaking with relief and peddled away to the comparative safety of her job. The Polish, of course, had no love for their occupiers.

Yes, Willi remembered, Lilly had talked about being a teacher, but decided on Red Cross training. He was proud and very enamoured of her in those youthful days. Then he also recalled that while Lilly was occupied thus, he was drafted into the German infantry on June 6, 1941.

Chapter IX
Going To Be A Soldier

Full of energy and enthusiasm, Willi and Lilly arrived in Germany committed to the changes in their new environments. They willingly joined their peers in the feelings of nationalism that swept through the ranks of German civilians and military alike. Each of them spoke Schwabish German and found the different dialects they encountered in their new surroundings difficult to deal with. With the resiliency of youth they adapted, but not without some frustrations. Willi relived his discouragements from a small isolated room in Vouziers, France.

"We were in camp where I was making furniture when I was drafted. The day was June 6, 1941. I was sent to Kemnitz in Saxon for my training. I got there and I didn't understand one single word they were talking about, the way they talked the German in Saxon. I couldn't understand them a word. I was just like a dummy. For about three weeks, until I woke up and thought,

'You better learn something before they kill you off here.'

"There was such a difference between dialects. I don't know how I learned... dumb like an ox. After you listen for a while you get it. We only knew the Schwabish German. You know Russia has 77 dialects; Germany has, I suppose, about 25.

"Most of my friends were already in the service. I do not know why I was later. Maybe I felt like I belonged there too. I don't know. I can't really tell you. You had to be healthy to be in the service. That was No. 1. I know people got rejected who were not 100% healthy or had bad teeth or so. They felt miserable in this age. Yes, I was happy to belong there, but I never was patriotic,

I mean political, because I wanted nothing to do with politics.

"No. 1 they taught us discipline. The German soldier was the most disciplined soldier in the whole world. When you had an order you had an order.

"For the first six to eight weeks in basic training you could not leave the campus beyond the gate. Of course, they had a job for you. Every second day or so you had to stand guard in front. They always find something for you to do.

"The training was hard. We had to learn to walk and to march. We had to walk five miles in a certain time. We had to run and that kind of stuff.

"Then shortly, I was sent to Berlin. There I had to go through interpreter's school. Lilly visited me because we were already engaged. She had with her a lady friend of her mother's. Lilly was in Weisbaden in school. She was thinking to be a Home Ec. teacher then, but changed her mind later. I remember she would not let me come close to her!"

Willi smiled to himself as he prepared for bed. What a girl that Lilly was... she had captured his attention away from the books alright! Tomorrow would be busy work with the Frenchman's son. As his head hit the pillow he hoped that thoughts about when he entered the infantry might put him to sleep.

Willi was soon called from school to active service.

"In time I was working in an office and lived in the barracks. Every single day I went to the movies in town. Sometime we went for a beer. Then I worked at Dresden as a bookkeeper and taking phone calls. Lilly visited me there too. I was there until early March 1943 until I was sent to Russia with my military unit. We were at Nicoliev, right on the Black Sea close to Odessa. It was very cold. Here we would jump into the river for a bath every morning and run two miles. I remember a beautiful bridge at Voznesensk. It was so sad when that beautiful bridge was destroyed.

"Later, on a bridge at Krivojrog I could've been killed. This bridge was at a point where I had to interpret for all three, Rumania, Russia, and Germany. It was by the border in each direction. The company was across the bridge over the Bug River. I was going toward the bridge and there came a guy toward me on a motorcycle. He warned me not to go over the bridge. He said it was too dangerous. I didn't listen to him and as I approached it, it went up in the air. Good thing I was not on there, otherwise I would not be here today either. That was probably my biggest scare in Russia. I never shot a bullet myself all the time in Russia. My job was to deliver mail, when I was not going to interpret.

"Then we started out towards Moscow. I went along with the troops to Kiev and all along the line until the Russians pushed us back in the winter of 1943. We were surrounded by them. Then we went to Munich in November and that's when I got leave to go to Poland and get married in January."

This tumultuous time was the background for the courtship of Lilly Mayer and Willi Winger, beginning in Rumberg and Schluckenau and continuing in Poland. They were engaged for four years. Willi wrote from Berlin to instruct Lilly to get marriage papers ready for a holiday wedding during Christmas time. When he arrived in Poland on furlough, blood tests and German citizenship papers were quickly arranged so that the wedding bans could be posted.

The wedding took place at Bergstatt, Poland, with Willi's uncle, Gotthold Winger, performing the ceremony. It was a joyous community celebration of three days at Niederland with a German band of eight soldiers providing entertainment. Marie helped with party arrangements and there was homemade wine for all. The wedding gifts from this celebration were eventually lost in Poland.

Even though Willi attempted to ignore the politics of those times, they were most definitely directing the course of his life. When the war began in September of 1939 with the German attack on Poland, Hitler had a substantially mobilized army. Germany had organized its plants for industrialization of war-time needs. The famous Wehrmacht, or armed forces, consisted of 106 combat divisions with tanks, motorized vehicles, and heavy artillery. As each of the Allies entered the war, they were not as well prepared or trained as the Germans. The Allies had to draft men and train them, transform factories, and develop strategies. Germany had 12,000 military aircraft, compared to about 8,000 for the Allies. The Allies, on the other hand, had larger navies, but had to patrol wide areas of the world, whereas Germany could restrict its fleet activities to the North Sea and the Atlantic. In addition, German submarines were a serious threat to Allied vessels carrying troops and war materials. From the time Germany attacked Poland until Japan surrendered six years later, the Axis powers mobilized about 30 million men and women. The Allies mobilized about 62 million. Willi and Lilly were entangled in this great global conflict.

Early in the war the Axis gained major conquests with the help of Italy, Hungary, Rumania, and Bulgaria. Hitler attempted to bomb Britain into surrender. When that didn't work, he turned to Russia.

The British repeatedly tried to warn Russia of signs they recognized that Hitler was planning to invade Russia in spite of the non-agression pact that he had signed in August of 1939 with Russian leaders. On June 22, 1941, more than 150 German and other Axis divisions swept across the Russian border in Operation Barbarossa. This 3-million-man invasion faced 2 million Russian troops. The battle line stretched 2,000 miles from the Arctic to the Black Sea.

Hitler told the world he had ordered the attack "to save the entire world from the dangers of Bolshevism." In truth, Germany needed Russia's vast resources. The Germans were confident, but were not prepared for the harsh Russian winter.

For almost five weeks, the Germans drove the Red Army back. The Russians destroyed or burned factories, dams, railroads, food supplies, and everything they could not move as they retreated. In October of 1943 the German army was surrounded in Moscow during a bitter cold spell. Willi was part of the Command Post Unit stationed there, just behind the front lines.

"Ya, this is when the Russians killed Germany, so to speak. I was there with the Ostkomenduntur, the big guys (meaning Command Headquarters). I always went with them along; however, they moved forward, you know. Then in November, 1943, we moved back to Nicoliev. From there on we had a call back to Munich. I was there a year and a half.

"Every time we got into a new town, we had a meeting and so I had to interpret the whole thing for the general or whoever made the speech. Same thing for the Rumanians wherever we are going. Besides, I answered the telephone, taking care of commands given from one group to the other group. I had a few jobs. Then I was assigned to a Russian captain, who had been a German prisoner. Later he joined up to our army. We had to take the mail from Nicoliev way to the front.

"Because I was assigned to this Russian-turned-German captain, I had good quarters. For some reasons he had all over friends and he took me with him to the Russian public. They fed us good and gave us to drink, more or less like family. I was very pleased and that guy thought everything of me too. We were very good friends. Of course, he was 40 years older than I was.

"One night we came back and it was dark already, maybe 7 or 8 o'clock. The Ostcom, about 30 or 40 people, were celebrating by a barrel of vodka there. Soon as we came in there came a big glass of vodka for each of us and we were thristy. I could not lift my head for three days. After that I could not smell vodka anymore!

"This particular evening we had a sergeant and he was a mean devil. So he got drunk too, very drunk. Next morning, he didn't even move any more. So what did we do? We got a casket and put him in the casket and made a picture of him in the casket and sent it to his wife."

The cleverness of his companions and himself caused Willi to laugh aloud and the sound of it reminded him of the reality of his present companionless state. The room he occupied had no bars on the single window and no locks on the door, but nevertheless it was a cage. His thoughts returned to the photo of the sergeant in the casket... pretty mean trick; so he and his buddies had written on the back side of the picture,

"He's still alive!"

It was war, but Willi's humor was always present. His philosophy was that one never knew the next day if one were going to be alive or not, but if alive one was obligated to have fun.

Willi, living as a soldier, and Lilly, as a Red Cross worker, were blown about like pieces of chaff in this global storm that wreaked its havoc on the land and on the hearts of generations to come. They escaped death while others succumbed to bombings, massacres, epidemics, and starvation. In the midst of this turmoil they had no news of each other or other members of their families.

On the threshold of their romance the two had not allowed the gigantic shadow of World War II to cast a blemish over their private world, but soon it couldn't be avoided. After six months of wedded life, from January to June of 1941, they were separated by a soldier's duty and they were not reunited until 1947 by letter. It was '1948 before they lived together again as a family. Willi was rembering their wrenching farewell scene as he rolled over in bed.

So, Willi was saying goodbye to Lilly in Poland as he fell asleep in France.

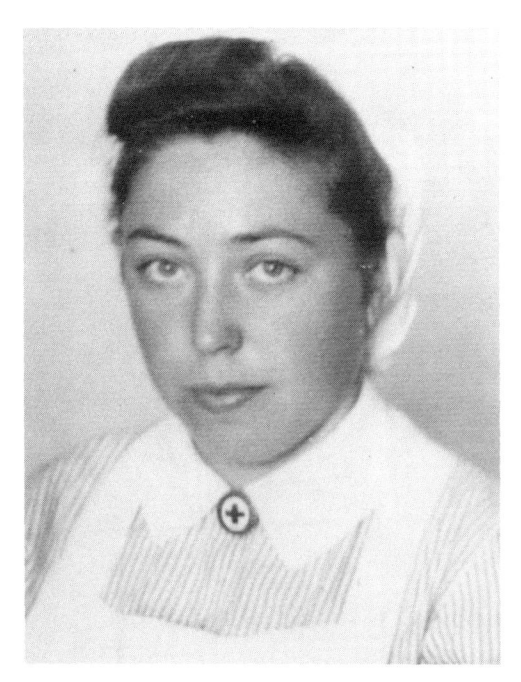

Lilly in Red Cross uniform.

Lilly Mayer and Willi Winger, Berlin, 1942.

Winger Wedding, January 6, 1944, Bergstatt, Poland.

Leo Mayer, 1969.    Wife of Leo Mayer, 1969.

Chapter X
On the Road Again

While Willy was occupied with his duties as a soldier, Lilly was at Jarocin, Poland, pregnant with her first child. It was as comfortable as life could be with the gloom of war on one's doorstep. Polish people had been put out to be replaced by Germans. Lilly found papers in the attic of the Polish farm house the Mayers now occupied. The name on them was Walter Herman. She thought to herself that someone's misery is somebody else's joy. The Mayers had livestock, chickens and turkeys, and registered horses. Nathanial Mayer purchased a mare and promised the colt to Lilly. When the foal was born, Lilly named it Felada. Felada occupied the place in Lilly's heart where Lady used to be. These good times were not long to last.

When the Russian advance moved toward Poland, the Mayer family became nomads once again. The captive, innocent life in the womb was oblivious to the turmoil into which it was about to be set free. During this time, Lilly had no news of her husband's assignments.

"We had to flee from the Communists. It was January 1945. I remember we had a Christmas tree still up. The tanks, the Panzers were coming. And the planes . . . it was terrible. We took two wagons. We had a family, a lady with a child I kind of adopted where I was working. She was from Lithuania and lived next to us. She had no property and no husband. In Poland there were many refugees besides us, from Estonia, Latvia, and other places."

Like thousands of other young girls, Lilly's robust dreams were affected by the ruinous hand of war. She tucked them into the recesses of her lioness heart and she ran, with her father and mother, with others seeking survival, and with the added responsibility of a new unborn life to protect. In spite of the destructive military climate where surroundings, relationships, and sometimes the human spirit could be sterilized or even annihilated, a seedling family took root and tried to make the best of it.

"So we were Mother, Father, the mother and child, and me pregnant... five of us. My brother Leo was in the service in Russia.

"Just that day we had butchered a pig and Papa was making the sausage. It was just done when the mayor came and said that in one hour we should be on the highway. The Communists were closing in on us. So we took gunny sacks, put sausage in there and put it on the wagon. Of course, we couldn't take much because we needed food for the horses. We packed that and took a little buggy and we put in everything important.

"To think of gunny sacks reminds me of the family who had their old grandma in the wagon. She was so sick and it was cold. When she died they put her in a gunny sack by the side of the road for the night. There was nothing else they could do. The next morning she was gone. Somebody thought the sack was full of food. They never saw their old one again.

"Ya, it was cold and we couldn't stop for fires, so I put the sausage between my legs to heat it up for eating. One evening we stopped at a deserted farm to make some coffee. The people had evacuated but some cows were in the barn. I thought some milk would be nice in the coffee. I go in the deep stall and got a few drips of milk from the cow. I moved to the next one and felt around. It turned out to be a bull! No milk there!

"Anyway, we flee then. We were headed into Germany, to Markröhlitz in Saxon, Germany, first stop from Poland. That's where Sig (Siegfried) was born on April 14, 1945.

"Before I had my baby, I remember the nights. There was an oil refinery where trains came to pick up the oil. The Americans knew exactly by the minute when the train was full. They dropped "Christmas Trees" (phosphorus flares) to see what's below. The bombs came and knocked everything down and it was at night always. The air was so thick you couldn't breathe and we had to run into the cellars and lay flat on the floor to pick out the clean air to breathe.

"My father worked for the lady where we stayed. One day he was plowing and the Americans and the English came down with regular shotguns from airplanes. He ran under the wagon and was safe, but they killed the horses."

There was a trail of lost horses in Lilly's life. To the loss of her pet, Lady, in Rumania, and horses at the Galatz port as well as these horses, Lilly could add Felada, who had to be left behind. Felada had eased the pain of separation from her husband during these troubled times. It was another lesson in steely resignation. She was always leaving behind her, somewhere, horses, those beautiful symbols of her Rumanian childhood.

"The Germans were shooting against the Russians and the Russians against the Germans and we were right in the middle of it in Markröhlitz. But it was quiet the day that Sig was born...about two weeks early.

"My girlfriend and I went for a little walk. There came planes that started shooting. We both got scared and started running. She was holding me on the arm. I thought I'd go this direction and she wanted to go that direction. She jerked me so hard and that night the baby started coming.

"It was the first baby and I was in terrible pain and the baby didn't come. So it was the whole day toward night when my father said, 'I can not take it anymore!' That town didn't have a doctor. So he took a bike and said,

'I'm going to the front. If something happens to me, it happens.'

"So on the bike, he got stopped by the American army. See, they were coming in already, the Americans. He was asked where he was going. He said my daughter is having a baby and there is no help for her. He was looking for a doctor. There was an American intern. He couldn't speak

German, but his male nurse was Jewish and could speak German. He said,

'Okay, I go along.'

"He came, you know, but he was almost too late for the baby. The baby didn't move anymore. The intern and male nurse didn't have nothing else but bandages. He went in and put a bandage around the little neck and pulled it out. There was no life. The baby was all blue and didn't move; so he took him by his feet and hit him so hard. I cried so much. Finally, the baby snapped out and screamed. So that's the way my Sig was born.

"Anyway, that American intern came back the next day. We had very little to eat and he brought a big pail, like the American army had, full of jelly for soldiers, and two big loaves of white bread. And I still think I have the little card he brought me with his name. It had a butterfly on it and he signed it.

"So the baby got very sick. When we traveled in January and February, I didn't get sick, but the cold went in to the baby like a blood poison. The baby broke out in blood pimples. It was pussy blood. He had such a high temperature he couldn't breathe anymore. We gave him baths in chamomile tea. We boiled rhubarb for the juice to give him and also boiled oatmeal and strained it for him. He slowly got better.

"We were occupied by the Americans when Germany was took over in May at the end of the war. Then Germany was divided in four parts for the English, French, Russians, and Americans. Our part of Germany was under the Russian tanks and ammunitions. So after we were occupied from the Russians, one day two Russian soldiers came and I don't know how they found out that my father could speak very good Russian. We didn't know that. They just came and arrested him and took him along. Of course, Mother was crying and I was crying.

"We didn't know what happened to him for four days and four nights. So one evening he comes back and he was white as a sheet and hungry. They had him for translating between the Russians and captured Germans. They let him go again. He didn't know why. They just directed him without saying. So anyway, that was a nice day when he came back again.

"We had two rooms there; I had one room and my folks had one room, on a farm with a German lady whose husband was a soldier too."

As in Willi's case, the dark circumstances that held Lilly and her family captive contained lighter moments.

"Our German landlady was a husky one. One day the Russian soldiers came.

"Shortly before they came, a garage door had hit against a chicken and broke its neck. She took it and threw it to the side to take care of it later. It didn't take too long and the Russian soldiers came. They want eggs and chickens. She didn't understand them, so she called to me to translate.

'Come down!'

"So I came down and I explained to the soldiers, 'No eggs, no chickens.'

"So what they did, they took the step ladder and went up where the hay is, looking for eggs. And she went into the house and got the shot gun. They left their guns at the bottom of the step ladder. When she got her own she said,

'If you don't come down, I will shoot you down! You can have that chicken.'

Lilly jabbed with her finger and continued,

"She pointed to the dead one by the garage. She was a 'woman's libber' before her time. Her husband was such a long time soldier and she had that farm to run all by herself. She wasn't so scared as we were. We were more afraid because of what we went through.

"Then Willi's oldest sister, Hilda, made papers for us. See, she did not go to the camp at Rumberg. She went directly to Wiesbaden. She was like a nun, a Lutheran deaconess. Anyway, she sent these to us in the Russian zone. We were from the German section what got cut up from the war. These papers say to let us go into the American side. We had papers. I left to go across the border into West Germany. I left by train with my son and some other ladies while my father took horses and wagon and wanted to go across the border. By the border the German Communists took everything... away... again.

"My folks had to walk after that...

"Sig and I came to Stuttgart by train and the German government put us in a camp again and every day I went looking for my folks. I looked all over and found them at the train depot. I took them along with me to the same camp. I don't remember how long we were in there. In 1946 we were sent by train to Pommertsweiler. Somewhere, somehow in this mess, my father lost his papers and that is why he had to get his birth certifcate from America where he was born."

At Pommerstweiler Lilly's father worked for the county cutting ditch hay. When the Wingers knew where the Mayers were located, they requested to go there also. The girls took work on surrounding farms and Alfred found employment with a trucking company. Lilly continued,

"Eventually, we were all reunited there; Willi and his folks too. I saw my brother's name on a Red Cross list and went to see him in the hospital near Munich. We had lost touch with him for so long. He wasn't a prisoner with my parents and me because he got sick in the Russian zone and got sent to Germany to the hospital because of his yellow jaundice. When we saw his name, it was a happy day.

"I had to take care of my baby and I had nothing, no income. I had 45 marks from the German government for the baby. Nothing for me. I worked for a beauty shop making hair nets."

The role of Lilly's family unit and millions of others was reflecting the political structure of each damaged nation. No one nation or family was spared. As nations compromised and regrouped, so did families. Reconstruction for the Mayers and their young daughter with a baby and no husband began as each nation attempted to repair the damage to its soil, its collective psyche, and its people. A new era was about to enfold. Just below the horizon, the nuclear family was awaiting its time to shine as post World War II households attempted to adapt to whatever was to be determined by the Allied and Axis Powers.

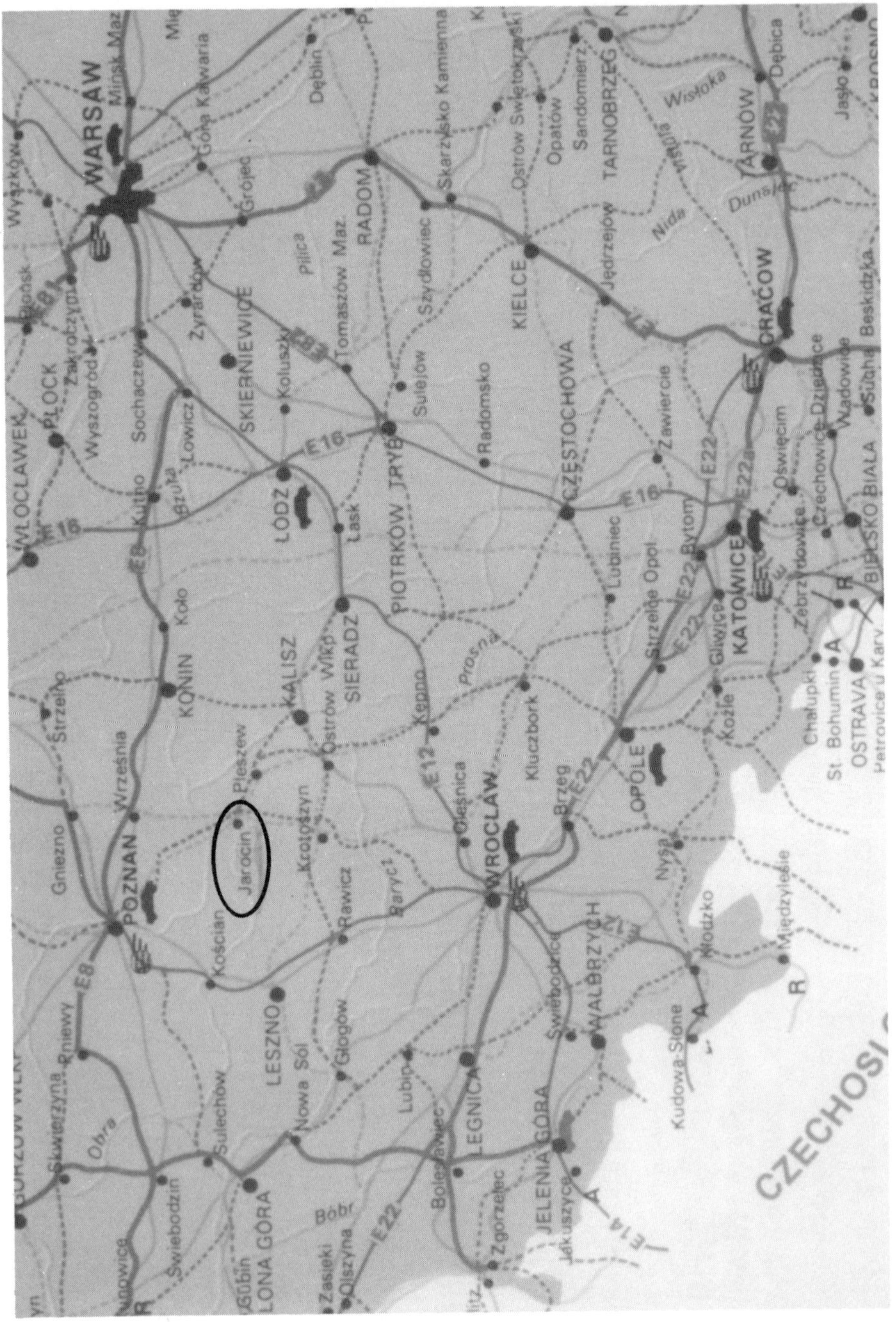

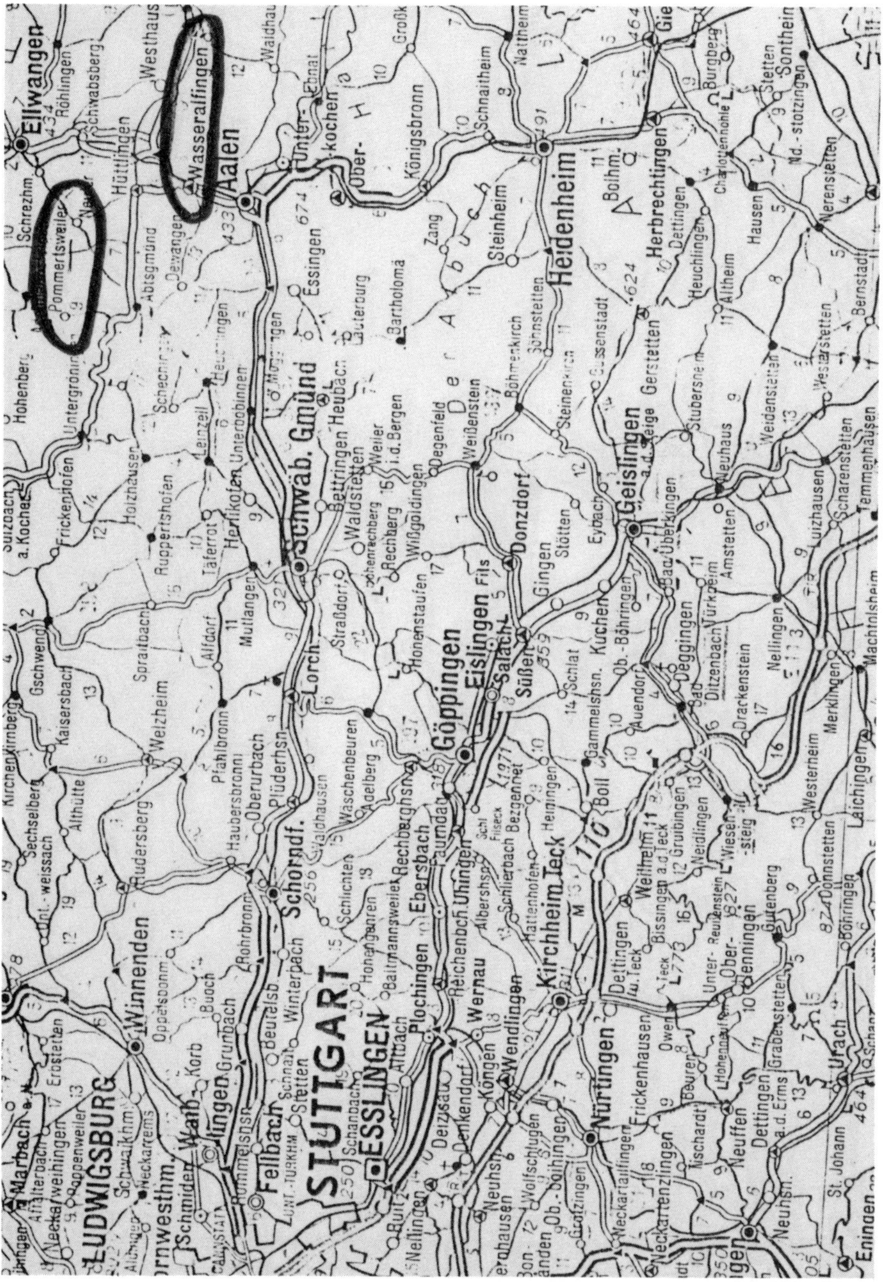
Ellwangen
Wasseralfingen
Pommertsweiler
Aalen
Schwäb. Gmünd
Heidenheim
Herbrechtingen
Göppingen
Eislingen
Donzdorf
Geislingen
Lorch
Schorndf.
Winnenden
LUDWIGSBURG
STUTTGART
ESSLINGEN
Fellbach
Plochingen
Kirchheim Teck
Nürtingen
Neuffen
Urach
Laichingen

Chapter XI
Farewell To Arms

The young Wingers corresponded through 1947 and the spring of 1948 while Willi was on the work program at Buzancy, France. After he had been there about seven months, he was allowed a visit home. Then he first met his son, who was now two years old.

At the termination of World War II, approximately the same time Willi was "catching a bullet with his foot," Lilly and their son, Sig, and Lilly's parents were in Markröhlitz, Saxon, Germany. From there Lilly had taken the train to Pommerstweiler, where they were when Willi came to be reunited with them when he was released on furlough from work duty in France. It was during this time, when countless people were attempting to restore their lives and homes, that correspondence was initiated between Lilly's family in Europe and those in the United States.

To be without papers during the aftermath of the war precluded almost any kind of travel and created much anxiety. In the melee, Nathaniel Mayer's birth certificate turned up missing, so contact was made with his uncle August Schaeffer at McClusky, North Dakota, U.S.A. Nathaniel had been born near Menno, South Dakota, in America, and then emigrated with his family to Russia when he was six years old. Lilly and her parents hoped that these American relatives could assist them in locating a copy of Nathaniel's birth record in South Dakota so he could obtain the necessary documents in Germany. An uncle and his wife, Lloyd and Tillie Houstman, who lived on a farm at Turtle, North Dakota, would be sponsors of an invitation to America during this correspondence.

Leo, who could read English, translated these letters to the rest of the family when they arrived. And because he was the first born, he had the first chance to accept the invitation to go to America. The sponsors in America could not afford to send for all of them. Events in Leo's life affected his decision. Lilly remembered her brother's disappointment.

"Of course, Leo was very much disappointed. He was 36 years old when he finally got married. He had been engaged when he was a young man in Rumania and she was a beautician. And they were very busy and it was warm, so she opened the door and made a draft. She was sweating and standing by the door to cool off. And she got a big chill and the same day she fainted, her lungs collapsed and she passed away.

"Leo took it very bad. So he couldn't decide for another woman so soon, you know. Of course, then in Germany he met his wife, but she did not want to go to America."

Willi nodded in agreement.

"She said absolutely NO. So there was our chance to take Leo's place, Lilly and me. We were right ready to go. There was not one thing in this world that could hold us up."

By providing this information, Lilly and Willi seemed to be silently speculating that if things had been different for Leo, it would have been he and his family going to America, not theirs.

Leo's story added drama to this episode in the Winger situation. When Leo had been discovered by his family in the hospital at Bayern near Munich, he was recuperating from severe yellow jaundice. He had been kept from active duty at the Russian front because of his slow recovery. After he regained his health, he courted and married Lilli Jachel at Unterkochen. These young people acknowledged the post-war renewal and the renewal of Leo's health by their marriage on September 24, 1949. When Leo's wife refused the American invitation, Willi and Lilly snatched at the opportunity to leave the devastation of war and its aftermath behind them. Willi had responded to Lilly from France after being informed of the American invitation, "Let's go tomorrow; let's get out of this hell. I don't want to see nothing from Europe anymore!" Their separated lives came full circle and closed on the past as they faced the future together. Of course, with this new set of events came another kind of separation, that of departing from siblings, extended family, and for Lilly, from her beloved mother. In the meantime, much effort and energy were required to mend their marriage and mold their reunited lives.

Chapter XII
Reunion and Repair

In 1947 Willi was required by the French government to return to work for another year under the prisoner exchange labor program. He fulfilled these duties and was released for good in October of 1948. To support his wife and child he took employment wherever he could find it.

"In a couple of weeks, there was a guy from Schlesheim who worked in a Wasseralfingen factory where they made American cars and trucks over. That guy helped me then to get a job. After the vehicles were repaired they came into a room where they got sprayed with paint.

"The fumes on the painting job gave me allergies and my ears swelled up so bad and my eyes. No matter what the doctor gave me, nothing would help. I had to take a bus to Wasseralfingen. My mother, sisters, and brothers, except for Alfred who was in Aalen, were in Pommerstweiler, 20 miles away. Lilly had just one room with our boy, Siegfried. I was there about a year and then found work with wood in Kessler's factory making crates and boxes. Oscar got work in a cast iron place.

"I had to work the whole night making crates etc. I left in the evening; it was 20 miles. I got sick of this, then came something else up. I got a job in Ulm. So then I could work in a furniture factory, but the problem was I could not find a place to live. That was 100 miles from Pommerstweiler."

During this period of struggle and renewal, a second son, Edgar, was born to symbolize it. The date was August 24, 1949. Besides this lively addition to the family, the letters and plans about going to America made time pass quickly. Then Willi was full of robust enthusiasm.

"The immigration officials asked all kinds of questions like, where we are, where we are going, why we want to go, who sponsors us, what kind of work, is there any sickness in the family, how many children . . . and oh, that poor little boy, Edgar. By now, we have another wonderful boy. He was two and one-half years old and was dragged from one office to the next when we went to Bremerhafen. He was standing and sleeping, but Sig was by now seven years old, so he was bouncing around already."

World War II had forced millions of people from their homes between 1939 - 1945. When the Communists took Rumania, 12 million Germans were expelled to Germany, including the Winger and Mayer families. Czechs and Poles moved onto the lands that these Germans vacated. Later, during the 1950's, thousands of anti-Communist migrants fled Russian-dominated countries in Europe and many more wished to find escape from the turbulent consequences. A mass of humanity began to shift and a bulk of it came to the threshold of America.

The Displaced Persons Act of 1948 and 1950 allowed 400,000 persons from Europe into the United States. Quota laws were then revised by the Immigration and Nationality Act of 1952 qrouping all prior legislation into one statute. This act limited quota visas to 154,657 per year. However, this number was raised by Presidential order to 158,361. Then in 1965 the quota system was abolished.

It was during the 1950's when the quotas were being adjusted that Willi Winger and his family first stepped upon North American soil. The 1965 Annual Report, Immigrations and Naturalization Service, U. S. Dept. of Justice, showed that the most immigrants received by the United States between 1820 and 1965 were German. The figure listed was 6,845,000 of which the Winger family were four, arriving in 1952.

United Nations Relief and Rehabilitation Administration, many private agencies, and the World Churches of America assisted people who were uprooted by the mighty struggle of World War II. One effort was to aid with transportation. The *General Hershey* was converted from a military vessel to a ship conveying a cargo of seekers who dreamed of economic and political freedoms. Willi and his family were some of those dreamers who booked passage on this ship. He explained a mix-up concerning who was to sponsor his family.

"Actually, we were sponsored by Uncle Lloyd Houstman, but for some reason he didn't have the money to send to New York, so Adolph Schaeffer sent it. That was another God-given idea, how we came to Bismarck, because otherwise they would have put us on a farm somewhere. Everything worked so beautiful, so wonderful, that sometimes you think if you wouldn't be religious, you would be the dumbest fool the world would ever have."

Willi's ability to accept the small triumphs in life and turn them into major accomplishments revealed his natural optimism. He had an almost uncanny talent for letting the good in and keeping the bad out.

Chapter XIII
Shaping Up and Shipping Out

Camp living was nothing new for the Wingers. As with the other times in their lives, they made the best of it at Bremerhafen where 1600 people who were emigrating were screened before being allowed to leave. The Wingers spent approximately six weeks there. While waiting, Lilly was full of anticipation for better days.

"They asked so many questions, but the nicest thing was when they asked us if we are without a job, are we going to be a burden to the government. So we said no; and that's when they agreed to let us go. For us to get to America was all handled through a church. The Nazarene Church sponsored everything.

"Before we entered the ship they told us that we can not take more than $25.00 money on the ship. We had money in Germany, so what did we do? We bought all kind of junk what we really didn't need to get rid of the money because we could only take $25.00. We bought a photo camera for over 500 marks which we didn't need just to get rid of our money. They gave us a paper that said so much money, jewelry, luggage, etc."

It was just another way of losing things.

Therefore the journey began. And now the despair which overwhelmed Willi's heart on the road near Bad Kreuznach and during the bad times at Sedan was replaced by hope as he and his loved ones began the pilgrimage to America. By an accident of circumstances, one of his captors was about to become his liberator. He was ecstatic.

"The nicest ten days of my life was on that ship. I had the greatest fun on that ship!

"It was the second day of May when we got on a bus and was shipped on the *General Hershey.* We were 1,600 people on that ship. See, they had no crew. They just had a captain. We had to cook, to serve. The people on the ship had to do all the work. There was just a captain and maybe a few mechanics.

"We were three couples who made friends. We just met in this camp. They were the Arthur Humans who now live at Wapata, Washington, and the Oscar Krauses who live in Colorado Springs, Colorado.

"Two days before we got on the ship, the ship people came and said they needed some cooks, they needed this and this and this. Oscar was picked for the kitchen. Human and me didn't get a job and that made us mad right away, because we didn't get a job. Krause said,

'You can be sure, you guys, we gonna' feed you guys. You never gonna' be hungry on this ship!'

"Okay, fine. So we got loaded. There was a nurse and everybody got two pills to take, probably for sea sick. She gave to me and I throw in the ocean and she was mad. I said,

'I'm not gonna' take a pill. You (meaning the nurse) can do whatever you want.'

"Now the ship went on a channel for two days. Now comes the nice thing.

"Of course, a very big mistake they did was the very first day they gave us food to eat. It was just incredible. Everybody was hungry and people ate like pigs. Okay . . . for one day. But the second day everything got out into the ocean into the fish! Ha!

"Now, our good friend Oscar, that guy, got so sick. The third day he could not even get out of bed anymore. So the third day from twelve guys in the kitchen, there was no one left. The whole crew was that sick. Now they needed us, me and Human and eight other guys. We were the only ten people on that ship what did not get sick on the whole trip. So now we were the cooks!

"But whatever we served, 80% went to the fish. They ate and then they throw it out again five minutes later."

Willi was delighted at the ironic turn of events that forced the original twelve cooks in the kitchen to relinquish their enviable positions of feeding the people to feeding the fish. He continued,

"Lilly got sick too, but she was not the worse one. Oscar Krause's wife, she was sick too, but not like him. One day Lilly was hungry and asked,

'Why don't you go down and make me a nice salad?'

"So I went down and tried to make a very good salad, real spicy, delicious, and I brought it up. One bite Lilly took and then no more. So Oscar Krause's wife ate the whole thing. She could do better than her man with the food!

"So we were ten days. I never in my life had so much fun just watching those sick people. We had music there and everything. And it was surprising toward evening, then we dance, then Lilly was alright; but as soon as morning came then she was sick again. But she was always okay in the evening for dancing. So we had a terrific time."

Not to be outdone by Willi's account, Lilly contributed.

"It was a Navy ship, you know, and the bathrooms were open. You could see the water. So when the little one was sitting on the stool there and the water splashed up, he jumped up and screamed. He thought he was going to drown!"

Lilly's animation increased as she continued to relate experiences on the ship.

"A lot of little kids were on the ship. They didn't have much toys. Boy, did I have a time chasing after them two. They were rascals. Willi couldn't help me because he was working in the kitchen for his buddy who got sick. We made picture of his buddy standing by the garbage can with his head over it!

"One evening it was so windy. See, the grown-ups had one dining room and I had to take the kids to a different dining room. And it was a very long table and kind of narrow. Anyway, the kids got their plates in front of them and they started eating. Then the ship went like that and the plate flew to the other end. And there they were sitting . . . with nothing and a fork!"

Willi resumed after the laughter stopped.

"We could not be together with our wives. We were separate. They were in one part and we were in the other. So nothing happens, you know. It was all open, you know. Just like the Navy. The children could be with their mothers."

Lilly carried on about the sleeping arrangements.

"We had two bunks. Sig slept on the top and me and the little one on the bottom. Sig was sea sick only one night; otherwise the boys weren't bothered much with it. Sig doesn't remember much of this."

The Wingers arrived at New York prepared to face the unknown once again. Homesick and seasick, Lilly was buoyed up by Willi's euphoria at the sight of the Statue of Liberty. Willi's happiness was like a dose of medicine that temporarily alleviated Lilly's aching heart and stomach. As if Liberty's arm were lifting them to heaven, Willi and his wife described their feelings as being "jubilized." (climbing up to heaven)

Willi appraised their entrance to a new country and a new period of adjustment with his usual candor and cool appraisal.

"So then we came to New York and we got unloaded. We didn't know it then, but soon after our arrival immigration was closed for three years. We took a train to Bismarck. We had lots of fun on the train. There were lots of people, not only us. Good food. We slept just by sitting."

Lilly added wistfully,

"You know, the kids were dirty, like piggies. And I was scared to death. At every little town they unloaded some people amd it got less and less of all that came over with us. It got darker and darker and more and more scary."

Willi finished,

"It was exactly a two day ride. 7:00 o'clock in the evening we stepped out in the Bismarck, North Dakota, train depot. Uncle Adolph and the pastor from the Church of Nazarene picked us up. It was a Friday evening, May 15, 1952, exactly seven years to the day when I was captured by the American soldiers."

Chapter XIV
Beginnings in Bismarck

For reasons unknown to the Wingers, train fare money was forwarded to them in New York City by Adolph and Martha Schaeffer of Bismarck, North Dakota, instead of the original sponsors, Lloyd and Tillie Houstman of Turtle, North Dakota. Both couples were relatives to Lilly's father. Here at the end of the American path for Willi, Lilly, and the boys there was a fork in the road. Instead of journeying to a farm at Turtle, they were routed instead to the city of Bismarck.

"So here we are," Willi took in air through his nostrils in a silent sigh, "and I got to say Aunt Martha was a most wonderful woman. To take people in that she never knew before and set us by the table and give us everything we wanted to eat."

The Wingers matched their memories which brought identical expressions to their faces.

"I remember what she had. Boiled eggs and weiners and potato salad!"

"We finished the whole table!"

"Not the table, the food!"

They were on a roll. Momentarily, they were maneuvering in their memories as if they were of one mind; however, Willi liked to get the last word.

"That first night in Bismarck our kids ate like hamsters. On the ship they threw out more than they ate!

"Aunt Martha took us upstairs. The apartment wasn't finished. We had a bed set and an apple box for a table. So we went to bed. It didn't last long . . . bang! The whole bed goes on the floor. Lilly was crying all night from lonesomeness and having a broken bed. Next morning we fixed it."

"Ya, we broke down the first night." But now, the tears Lilly had shed that night were long forgotten in a watershed of other sorrows put to rest by better days. "Lucky the kids had the rollaway."

Willi interrupted,

"We had $10.00. So the next morning, Saturday, I take the two boys and myself to the barber and it cost $5.00 and that left $5.00 for groceries."

Lilly fired details, like pebbles from a slingshot.

"I bought milk, bread, and butter and jelly. Bread was $ .18 a loaf and butter $ .60 a pound."

Willi nodded in agreement and continued,

"So, this was Saturday and then came Sunday and we went to Church of the Nazarene. Maybe this is not nice to say, but it was not what we were looking for. That yelling and that kind of singing so; it disappointed me very terrible. And we couldn't understand the English too good.

"Monday morning Uncle already had a job lined up for me. I went to work for a Mr. Reche. He was an electrical contractor and I never in my life touched electrical whatsoever. I didn't even know what was an electric wire. That man could not speak a German word and I could not do English. There we was with our hands. He showed me only once and I knew exactly what to do with outlets and switches. The biggest surprise was, yeah, what do I gonna' get paid. And that man was so sweet and nice. He paid me right away $1.50 an hour and that was good money in 1952. So I work for him for a whole month.

"And then comes Mr. Stude from the Hamburg area, 100% German who lives in Bismarck. He had Stude Millworks right on 9th Street. It was not very far to go to work and he was probably the best cabinet maker in North Dakota at that time. He was popular all over the state. I remember some stories he told. Like when they came and wanted him to buy war bonds during the war. He said,

'To hell with you guys, I'm not going to buy to shoot my brother!'

"Anyway, so Mr. Stude came out to the apartment and wanted me to come to work. I like my job with Mr. Reche, only one problem. The boss can not talk German and I no English. We just talk with our hands. I say to Stude,

'How much you gonna' pay me?'
'$1.00 an hour. All in my shop are getting $1.00.'
'Oh, no. I would not be dumb enough.'
"So we talked again the next day.
'$1.35 an hour!'
'Oh, no.'
'$1.50,' I demanded.
'What about the other guys in the shop?' he questioned.
'You can do whatever you want. I don't care. If you give me $1.50 an hour I come and work with you.'

"So I told Mr. Reche and I still feel bad today. The poor guy, he almost cried. He just don't want me to leave him. Only a month later, he had a heart attack and died. I hope it did not happen because I left him. He and his wife were so good to us. But I had to look out for the future, so I went to Stude Millworks. I worked there from June 15, 1952, to June of 1959, seven years.

"Then we started housing. And we had to pay back Adolph Schaeffer $214 for the train fare from New York. He had a hardware store in Washburn and was working on the side as a guard at the penitentiary. Our money was so little because at that time, they (camp authorities in Europe) were so gosh-darned crooked and told us rules that we were forced to follow. We had to spend our money from Germany."

Willy opened his mouth to say something more, but Lilly interrupted to explain further.

"I still have this watch we bought because I could have one watch along. Not once a repair. I had it appraised years ago. They said it was worth $250.00. It is all gold, but the band is wearing out. Anyway, we had to count the pennies in 1952 and 1953."

Keeping quiet for a moment, Willi was eager to share how he saved money for the family.

"At that time I was a smoker and we could buy a whole carton of cigarettes for $1.00. That was a year, I tell you. At 11:00 P.M. on March 26, 1954, I quit and never touched another cigarette. We celebrated Oscar Krause's birthday on that day. We smoked, and drank wine, and coughed a lot. The next day was my birthday and I had a headache so I said,

'The hell - - - no more of this!'

"Then I never touched a cigarette anymore. I mean, ya, I got smart." He paused, looked at his wife out of the corner of his eye and said,

"I'm still smart, got smarter."

Even though Lilly's face was full of mischievous thoughts, she just smiled and said nothing.

The Wingers had maintained their relationships with Oscar Krause and Arthur Human and their wives. Upon their arrival in North Dakota, Oscar had found work with the county of Burleigh doing road work and Arthur worked on a farm near Fredonia. Later he rented and bought land near Ashley.

Arriving in May the Wingers had not yet been introduced to North Dakota winters. Because funds did not stretch to cover the cost of a vehicle, Willi had to walk to work. On one occasion the newcomer was boldly nipped by Jack Frost.

"In 1953 we had a strong winter. I had no car, no nothing at first; so when I walked to work I didn't cover my head. In Russia and Rumania it didn't get so cold where we lived. So I froze my ears. I bought a cap after that. Then one of the buddies at work gave me a ride."

Besides adjusting to the climate, the family found some traditions in the American culture strange. Sometime later, when they did own an automobile, Lilly was amazed and perplexed by events on October 31.

"We had our first Halloween in America. We came out in the morning when we had our first car. It was 1954 and we had a 1952 Chevy. It was just sitting flat! All four tires empty! We didn't know the meaning of the garbage cans all over either. Our neighbors explained to us the joke about Halloween!"

Lloyd Houstman's father came to help Willi finish the apartment upstairs at the Schaffer place.

"It didn't take very long and it was very nice. We had two bedrooms, a living room, kitchen, and bath. We had a refrigerator and table and chairs. We were there three years and then bought our first home in 1955 for $7200 and remodeled. That's where the girls were born. Edith on May 3, 1955, and Ruth on August 9, 1959."

As a mature woman, Lilly was still experiencing new traditions and people, just as she had as a young girl in Europe. There she had the company of her parents. In America, she felt the separation from her parents strongly and was lonesome for them. Willi put it in simple words.

"Lilly was very homesick the first two years. Then in 1954 we brought her parents over and it was okay. For me, it was like stepping out in Germany one morning to work in the United States. It made just no difference whatsoever. I was at home right away. For her it was a different story. I never in my whole life was homesick, even as a soldier, I never was."

For some who are born and reared on ancestral ground, it might be difficult to understand that these people carried their home in their hearts. Their separate passages and their joint travels had initiated them to varied sites that were temporarily labeled home. Now, clinging together as a family of six instead of two, like a clump of dandelion seed blown about by the winds of war, its bruised, but tenacious seed settled lightly on the bed of free soil and began to take root, for the last time, in the city of Bismarck, North Dakota.

Chapter XV
Life As Citizens of America

Finding enough security to establish a home, the Wingers diligently began to search for added identity in order to contribute to the community which surrounded them. It was important for Willi to feel comfortable in church.

"After the second Sunday of church in the United States in 1952, we went to the Faith Lutheran Church in Bismarck and we been there ever since. At that time everything was German service yet. The Faith Lutheran is just around the corner, one block. They were 85 people before we joined. For two straight years I played the organ for every church service until I cut my little finger off in the shop. Then it didn't work anymore, the accordian the same thing. We gave the accordian to the oldest son. We brought it over, you know. I don't know what he did with it. It was very, very beautiful, from Italy."

Willi served as President of the Council of the Faith Lutheran Church in Bismarck in 1971 to 1972.

Full of energy and aspirations, Lilly took a job at the Baptist Nursing Home for the Aged as an aide. To work as a nurse she was required to take a state examination, but did not do so because of the language barrier. However, her German served her well as an aide because many of the residents at the Home spoke German. She was a valuable member of the Baptist Nursing Home staff for nine years. As mentioned earlier, during this time two more children were added to the Winger family. Edith was born in 1955, and Ruth in 1959. Because these girls were born in the United States, they spent their childhoods far from the fields and vineyards of their Rumanian parents.

These were good times for the Winger family. They became involved in the industrial workplace of America at a time when an unskilled, uneducated white male had unlimited opportunities. Willi and Lilly used what training they had and made the most of it.

The couple's exuberance about this period in their lives could be detected in Willi's voice.

"Three years before we became citizens of the United States we brought Lilly's parents over . . . March of 1954. They lived with us until her father died in June of 1956 and then, of course, her mother lived another eleven years after, until 1976. Since Lilly's father had been born in the U.S., he could collect social security because he had worked 18 months. He had a job with Schulz Creamery & Butcher Shop cutting meat and making sausage. Lilly's folks helped us out and we helped them.

"They spoke only German when they came. When Lilly was working they stayed with Edgar, when he was four or five or so. So Edgar had more of an adjustment to make when he went to school because he was not used to the English. Sig had one year school in Germany and then took first grade in America again."

The family arrived in May when school was dismissed, so Sig had the summer to learn the language by being with the children of the neighborhood. He did well in school. In spite of a difficult start, Edgar proved to be a good student later on.

Not only did the two boys assist their parents with their English, but also helped them with their studies to become naturalized citizens. Sig was approximately twelve and Edgar about eight years of age. Lilly was very nervous about the examination. When required to write a sentence in English, she wrote,

"It is a cloudy day."

It was a day to celebrate. The family had a big meal and speeches were made for friends and relatives. Lilly's cousin's wife, who worked at Buttrey's Department Store, gave clothes to Lilly. For this occasion Lilly vividly

remembered one of these gifts. It was a lovely red dress with black leaf embroidery. The boys even had little suits. Afterwards Willi walked around with his chest puffed out repeating to anyone who would listen,
"I think I'm going to like it here!"
It was May 15, 1957.
Being naturalized was the highlight of their lives until 1959 when the Wingers traveled to Germany and another little Winger was born to them. These two events created almost equal enthusiasm.
Willi reported on their adventure across the ocean.
"For a month in 1959 we took a trip to Germany. Number 1, it was exciting! We hadn't seen the families for seven years and, of course, my mother-in-law was with us. Her son was still over there. She had only two children, so she was happy to go.
"It was very amazing and surprising. They picked us up in Stuttgart. The whole family of about 35 people were waiting for us at the airport and when we came home to Pommerstweiler they had the whole house, everything, decorated with WELCOME. It was a very beautiful reunion."
Full of good will and pleasant memories, Lilly continued,
"It was March and I was pregnant with Ruth who was born in August. Our relatives teased me that I was gaining weight and I said,
'Well, we have good food in the U. S.!' " Lilly ardently gestured to show a big stomach.
It was a source of pride to Willi that he had saved enough American dollars to bring the entire family to visit in Europe.
"My mother was alive yet and all our brothers and sisters. It cost us $7,200 just for the air fare for the whole family, a very expensive trip. We rented the biggest Mercerdes in Germany and we traveled 2,000 miles around Germany with our rented car. It was a wonderful time. Lilly's mother stayed with her son, Leo, in Underkoeken. We went into Switzerland and Vienna and came home.

"On our way home from New York we met a couple. She was dying of cancer and came to the doctor in New York. They were flying back on the same plane, so we met them and two or three days later she passed away. That guy, through the death of his wife, had to stop all his finances. He had no way to go, but to sell. He had this lot here in Bismarck and that's how we got here.

"When Lilly's parents came from Germany we had bought an old house one block from Uncle's place on 15th Street where we had been in the apartment upstairs for about three years. My father-in-law helped us to remodel the house. We put new cabinets in and everything. We paid only $7,200 and sold it for $13,000.

"Myself, I spent everything in Germany, you know. I did not have even one hundred bucks. So I went down to the bank to get dollars to buy this lot from the man with the sick wife. I had a good friend there from before when I had wanted to buy Stude Millworks. I always wanted to buy his shop. It was a good business and the man was 72 years old already. So that time I went to the bank and the banker says,

'I give you $60,000.'

"But Mr. Stude was too proud and wanted $200,000; then six months later he passed away and his wife sold it for $30,000. I had wanted to give $60,000. That was lots of money at the time. That made me to want our own business.

"Anyway, I went to the same banker. I got a good deal here, I said. Somebody wants to sell me a lot for $2,200.

'Sure,' he said, 'here, you got it.'

"He gave me the whole money. I didn't have a penny. Six months later he gave me $22,000 to build the house on the lot. That time it was so easy. Now you can't do that. Just put your name on the paper, that's all."

A new house was built on the purchased lot 500 North 19th Street. HOME SWEET HOME IN AMERICA.

Winger family, 1965.

THE UNITED STATES OF AMERICA

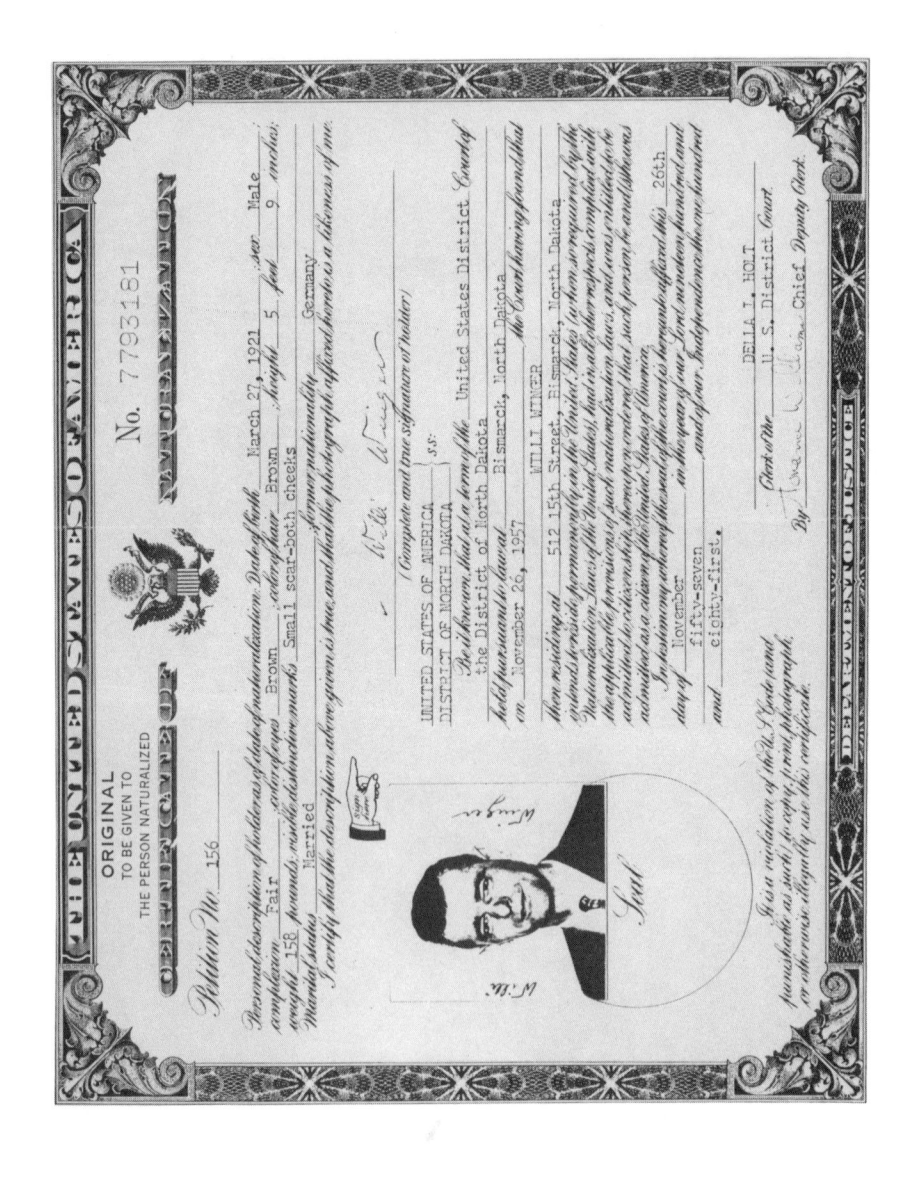

No. 7793181

ORIGINAL
TO BE GIVEN TO
THE PERSON NATURALIZED

CERTIFICATE OF NATURALIZATION

Petition No. 156

Personal description of holder as of date of naturalization: Date of birth March 27, 1921 sex Male complexion Fair color of eyes Brown color of hair Brown height 5 feet 9 inches weight 158 pounds visible distinctive marks Small scar—both cheeks
Marital status Married former nationality Germany

I certify that the description above given is true, and that the photograph affixed hereto is a likeness of me.

Willi Winzer
(Complete and true signature of holder)

UNITED STATES OF AMERICA
DISTRICT OF NORTH DAKOTA } ss:

Be it known, that at a term of the United States District Court of the District of North Dakota held pursuant to law at Bismarck, North Dakota on November 26, 1957 the Court having found that

WILLI WINZER

then residing at 512 15th Street, Bismarck, North Dakota intends to reside permanently in the United States (when so required by the Naturalization Laws of the United States), had in all other respects complied with the applicable provisions of such naturalization laws, and was entitled to be admitted to citizenship, thereupon ordered that such person be and (s)he was admitted as a citizen of the United States of America.

In testimony whereof the seal of the court is hereunto affixed this 26th day of November in the year of our Lord nineteen hundred and fifty-seven and of our Independence the one hundred and eighty-first.

DELLA I. HOLT
Clerk of the U.S. District Court.
By _____ Chief Deputy Clerk.

It is a violation of the U.S. Code and punishable as such to copy, print, photograph, or otherwise illegally use this certificate.

THE UNITED STATES OF AMERICA

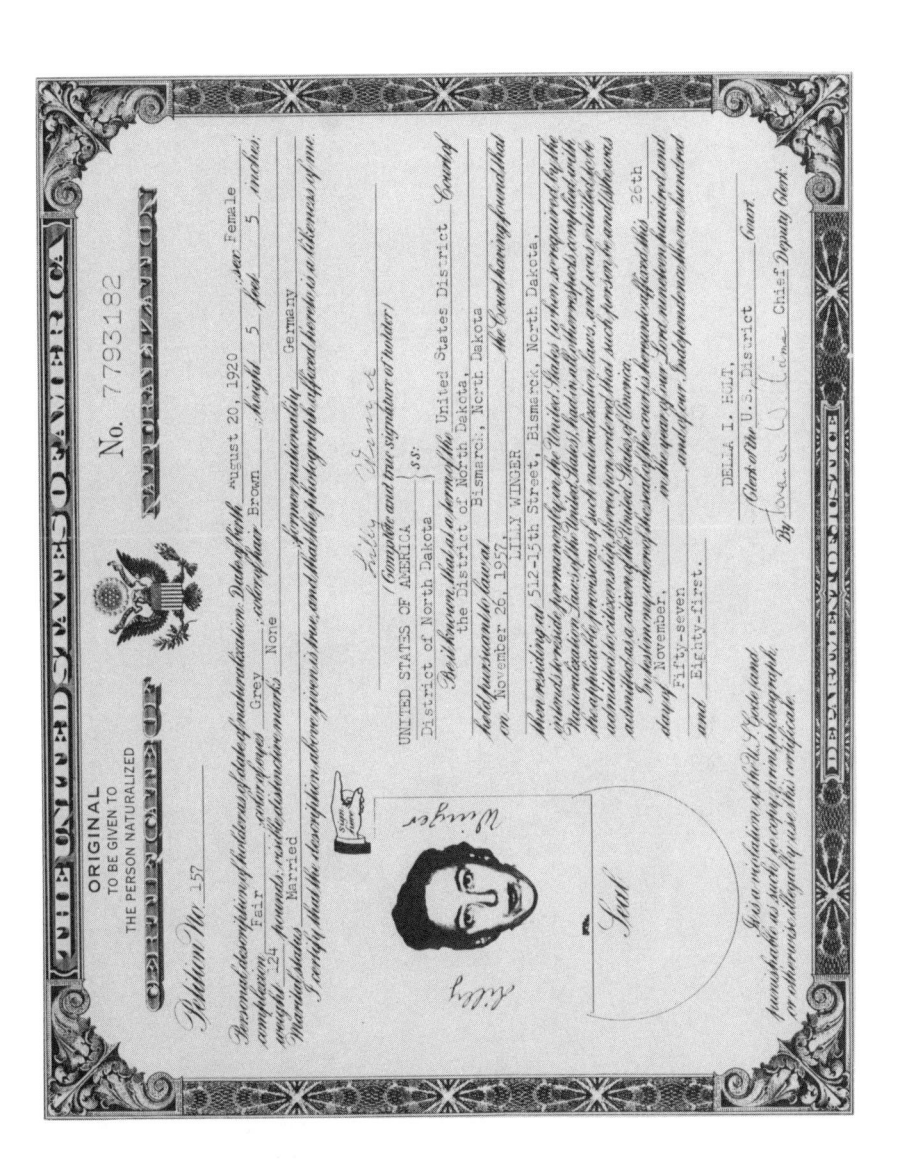

No. 7793182

ORIGINAL TO BE GIVEN TO THE PERSON NATURALIZED

CERTIFICATE OF NATURALIZATION

Petition No. 157

Personal description of holder as of date of naturalization: Date of birth August 20, 1920 sex Female complexion Fair color of eyes Grey color of hair Brown height 5 feet 5 inches; weight 124 pounds; visible distinctive marks None

Marital status Married former nationality Germany

I certify that the description above given is true, and that the photograph affixed hereto is a likeness of me.

Lilly Winger
(Complete and true signature of holder)

UNITED STATES OF AMERICA
District of North Dakota ss:

Be it known, that at a term of the United States District Court of the District of North Dakota, held pursuant to law at Bismarck, North Dakota on November 26, 1957, the Court having found that

LILLY WINGER

then residing at 512-15th Street, Bismarck, North Dakota, intended to reside permanently in the United States (when so required by the Naturalization Laws of the United States), had in all other respects complied with the applicable provisions of such naturalization laws, and was entitled to be admitted to citizenship, thereupon ordered that such person be admitted as a citizen of the United States of America.

In testimony whereof the seal of the court is hereunto affixed this 26th day of November, in the year of our Lord nineteen hundred and Fifty-seven and of our Independence the one hundred and Eighty-first.

DELLA I. HULT,
Clerk of the U.S. District *Court.*

By _____ Chief Deputy Clerk.

It is a violation of the U.S. Code (and punishable as such) to copy, print, photograph, or otherwise illegally use this certificate.

Winger's first car.

Chapter XVI
Building A Business

"So we built this house. The basement was all open space. I was comfortable and I knew everything that was going on. I started business on my own making cabinets in June of 1959 . . . pretty good thing, to start a business. We were the Winger Cabinet Shop. Two weeks later I hired one man to help me. So we worked in the basement for three or four months. My neighbors didn't like that and went to the city. They came and said,

'You gotta' go out of here, not a commercial zone, don't allow this here.'

"I had no choice. I had to rent. I found me a shop about eight blocks from the house. Very nice. A German guy, his name was Al Fetzer, gave me one-half a building. So I put my shop in there. I paid $150 per month rent for having a shop there for 15 years.

"Then we started out our business with no money, so I went down to the bank again and borrowed $10,000 for machines. Nobody asked a question.

"The first year we had only a income of $72,000 for a whole year. Of course, we were only two guys. Still not too bad. Then we hired four more people, so we were six. And by the second year we reached the income of $135,000. By 1970, I employed twelve people and our income was close to $400,000.

"In 1971 something slipped in my head (an idea occurred to him). Our mortgage payments on the house were only $114 a month. As soon as the neighbors chased me out, we made the downstairs into an apartment and we made $130 rent. So the rent was higher than the payment.

"Another guy came by in 1971 and said,

'Say, I've got here three beautiful lots. Why don't you buy them lots and you can build some apartments?'

"I had only $200 and each lot was $7,000. So down to the bank I go again... this time I need $21,000 to buy them. By October, middle of 1971, I bought another $75,000 and built three six-unit apartment buildings. Well, it was pretty good... $150,000... and two more six-plex units. We got a nice income. We never had one day vacancy in 17 years in our apartments. Not a single day. They are very wonderful people, age 62 and over. We are our own managers.

"Lilly took care of calls and customers when I was out of town. She would also look after problems with our employees and even helped to finish the woodworking. She was always helping with the business too.

"Then I bought my own building for the shop on the Expressway in 1974. I paid $85,000 and moved in there. Winger Cabinets did work all over North Dakota, South Dakota, and even Colby, Kansas.

"We had good business. I wanted to retire in 1983, but it didn't work out.

"So the end of being a cabinet maker comes on December 5, 1987, instead. Everything gone, except the building. So, now I had a building for sale. In 1983 we were fifteen people in the business. Now since December 15, 1987, we are retired."

Champion Auto business currently occupies Willi's former building in Bismarck. The moral of this story is that free enterprise speaks for itself.

Winger's Cabinet Builders.

Chapter XVII
Hurts and Healings

While the Wingers were rebuidling their personal lives after World War II, the forebodings of a cold war between communism and the free world were also building. As the Soviets replaced non-communist regimes with dictators, the United States took a dim view. Postwar Germany was quickly divided into communist and non-communist areas, and when the Western zones solidified, Russia blockaded Western Berlin demanding that the West leave. During the 1950's these two ideologies collided in Iran, China, Vietnam, and Korea. And so, as a small, free enterprise cabinet-making business expanded in Bismarck, North Dakota, USA, so did the global arms race.

As citizens in America danced to rock and roll, President Eisenhower attended the first conference since 1945 of the Big Four in Geneva. The Soviets launched Sputnik I in 1957, and the Americans followed with Explorer I in 1958. Nassar and Castro borrowed money and power from Khrushchev as DeGaulle renewed France.

Participating in World War II and the refugee experience left both Willi and his wife with a distaste for politics. About these matters Willi was firmly pessimistic, or as those who agree with him might prefer to say, realistic. The complexity of a war-abused existence and the sense of helplessness that accompanied it remained fresh in both of their minds.

"I don't want anything to do with politics! I did my duty only as a soldier in Germany. So did Lilly as a Red Cross worker. I am no better than a Russian, a Pole, or Frenchman, or American. We are all the same when it comes to war, regardless of who we are. There is only one principle ... killing and strafing (rake with fire at close range, especially with machine guns from low flying aircraft) ... even after the war is supposed to be over.

"The war was depressing and discouraging. We know some people don't believe us about what happened to us. Our children ask us questions and we talk to them. It was always my dream to write a book. Sometimes I can remember just like yesterday."

No one who lived in Germany before, during, or after the World War II years could escape the impact of political history, including, of course, Hitler's treatment of the Jews. Willi had mixed feelings about these events.

"The Jews in Germany were not treated right. By the time the war broke out that was all over with ... about 1933 - 1939. There were no more Jewish stores etc. We heard some things in Rumania, but we were too young to understand. We heard some stories that were mixed ... that their skills were squelched etc. In 1933, I was only 12. To be honest, we could care less, because at that time we never dreamed we would go to Germany.

"When we did come to Germany that was all over. There was no more such a thing as Jewish premises or stores. After that they took us from camp to put us on farms throughout Poland.

"When I was working as an interpreter, the Russians put a captured Jew to the side. I remember one time, our captain made a speech I had to interpret. There I found out that the Jewish people from this town were taken to Germany, not a prison camp in Russia. They were right away separated. I knew something was wrong, but not what ... when I was in Russia.

"When I was young, we had a Jewish store. When that guy needed somebody to work he always called on me. I even got a suit for half price. He was nice to our whole family. And the Commander at the American camp at Bad Kreuznach was Jewish. I had personally nothing against the guy. He was a big guy and I was a nobody.

Jewish people were my good friends in Bismarck when I had a business."

Lilly had remained silent through this entire monologue. However, now she cleared her throat as a signal that it was her turn to speak.

"See, Jewish people are known as business men and the German people borrowed money from Jewish people and then couldn't pay it back; so the Jewish people took away their buisness or their furniture or whatever, you know."

Willi agreed,

"We got quite a few Jews here in Bismarck. When I worked for Stude there was a Jewish contractor. Whenever he built a house he would not let anybody install the cabinets except me. That particular guy gave me a bonus of $100. So I enjoyed him and he really liked me. His name was Ben Markowitz. Nicest guy."

When Willi was a newcomer to America and because he had served in the German infantry and worn the uniform, he was sometimes a victim of discrimination himself during those post-war years when Americans were flushed with burning patriotism. He recalled the following event when he and Lilly had attended a wedding dance in Regan, North Dakota, during the late 1950's.

"The women were sitting upstairs and the men downstairs. We knew all them guys' whole families, you know. They were interested to know how it was in Germany . . . how we got to war and stuff. I was telling them and I mentioned the name Hitler a few times. There was a young guy in the Marines or Air Force. That guy stood up and said,

'Come on out here!'

"He was in a uniform and I thought he was going to kill me, so I said,

'Who in the hell are you?'

"And he said,

'I am an American Marine!'

"And then I said,

'To hell with you. I am an American citizen!'

"We almost got to a fight. One of the other guys came out and smoothed things over so we didn't fight. Then I learned that you better *shut up before you get into trouble*. I would not kill him, but I would have taught him a good lesson! I was never afraid of anything in my life."

Willi had a great deal of confidence in himself gained from his youth. His decision-making machinery was put into gear at age eleven with the early death of his father and he found great emotional support in his religious upbringing. He was always faithful to it.

"When I was in prison at France I started to go to the Catholic Church. I stayed there until the last Sunday I left the community. For me, it is not Sunday if I don't go to church. I don't want to sound fanatic, it's just my belief. It's a good part of my life. As far as financial, I want to do the best ever possible for me to take care of the church. Religious faith helped me through prison. It helped when the French people saw me in church praying like everyone else.

"I missed two Sundays in church my whole life time, taking out the five years of war. When there was war, there was no such thing like going to church as a soldier in Germany. Those two I missed were in the United States."

Willi attacked problems when they attacked him. His limited education in Europe was continued in America through the College of Hard Knocks, especially with his business. He rose to the challenge of the hurts and healings that came his way through the cabinet-making business.

"They didn't have very little union in North Dakota during my business days. I always paid my employees better than union scale.

"One time I went out to measure for cabinets and then we had Easter Sunday. On Easter Monday I go to the shop and all employees are standing outside. Nixon froze the wages. So they demand more wages.

"I called my secretary who called Fargo, so I couldn't give them a raise. So they didn't come to work. I said, 'Well, if you don't come to work, you just gotta' go home."

This was a time of domestic concern and inflation. Americans were earning more money than ever before but rising prices cut their gains. In 1971 President Nixon set up a Pay Board to stop inflationary wage and salary increases and a Price Commission to regulate price and rent increases. Business increased in 1972 and the inflation rate slowed, so he lifted the governmental limits in 1973. Willi attempted to make sense of the complicated patterns of supply and demand.

"I didn't fire anybody. They went to the union for help and the union boy said no. So four guys came back to work. Five left. Then I found out. The guys were not at fault. The guys did not want a strike. My own foreman arranged everything and blamed everything on the workers. So I said to him,

'You are going. You are fired. Get the hell out of here!'

"It took only a short while and two came back . . . and two new ones. After this, there never was an incident, because I always paid good wages. Things went on as usual.

"One time the penitentiary called and wanted to know if I would like to employ a cabinet maker that was in prison. He was really not locked up. The guard would bring him every morning and pick him up every evening. So I hired him.

"He was a good worker. I was very satisfied with him. So that went on for a month or six weeks. Finally one morning the guard brought him to the front door, the guard went, and the prisoner disappeared. They caught him three or four days later in Duluth, Minnesota.

"Now the penitentiary gave him a little tool box with some tools. I don't remember if he took it home with him every night or left it there. After he disappeared, the penitentiary called me and said,

'Where are the tools?'

"I didn't know anything. We had our own tools. Our own employees never had to buy their own tools. Anyway, they took me to court over them tools. I never had to pay a penny or anything, but them suckers took me to court.

"We found the tool box, but there were things missing. The judge threw the case out of court. The police chased this guy on a motorcycle and he fell down a ditch and was in very bad shape for a long time. I lost complete control, I mean touch, with him.

"Another incident of when I hired a guy — another man would always come to pick him up in a ministerial uniform. So I thought,

'Why does he always pick him up?'

"Finally we found out a hammer was missing and a saw was missing. Of course, I always went home for lunch and then he hid things under the shrubs. One evening I confronted him because we caught him picking things up. After this I fired him.

"It turned out he was one of those Satan Worshippers. So we questioned them. They told us their conscience was to kill people. Can you imagine? Of course, he was gone. This was in Bismarck in our shop in the early 1970's. Can you imagine? We didn't have him too long."

It appeared that democracy was at work at the Winger Cabinet Shop. Willi was working with people from all parts of the American society and was discovering first-hand how life and business operated under the Bill of Rights.

People in America were very verbal. In their personal lives the Wingers discovered that not all Americans were as thrilled with the presence of German immigrants as Wingers were. Lilly remembered the rumors about the second-hand dress she wore on the day she was to be naturalized. She supposedly traveled to New York City to buy it. Other prejudiced remarks were conveyed when Wingers gave opinions and money through church committees or when they vacationed in Hawaii to celebrate an anniversary. But these were petty social judgments that could exist anywhere and were considered spiteful, but not overwhelming in comparison to the past struggles the family had experienced.

Both Willi and his wife exhibited an expansive love for America. They have realized the American Dream. Willi Winger did not set out to pursue it, per se. In fact, as an enemy of the Allies he served against it. In the search for a worthy way to live, he found the opportunity and seized it. All four of the Winger children have been college-educated. The family owns a lake home and has the means for travel and enjoys the privileges of security and comfort. Willi and Lilly think of their birthplace, but do not long for it. Lilly expressed her feelings with only a trace of melancholy.

"It's always the place where you were born... but it's communist. I don't know if I want to visit. I haven't got no trust in Europe. There is always something going on. I'm afraid to get stuck in there. Something could happen so I couldn't get out no more."

She was pensive, but not sad. Willi showed his usual aloofness.

"I am a completely different person than most people. I never in my life got homesick. Only time I really was bitter was when they shipped us from Germany to France when we were supposed to go home. They treated me so terrible in France that I could probably kill every Frenchman. But besides this, I never was bitter against anybody or nobody. I believe in forgive and forget. I mean, you can make me today mad like everything and tomorrow I even don't think about it."

Beaming at the grass roots, a Rumanian ember rests with the Winger name in middle-class, mid-western America. Like a meteor chip it was catapulted by outside forces to Czechoslovakia, to Germany, to Poland, to Russia, and back again; finally to move, this time by inner forces, to America. Granted, its small pinpoint of light may be overpowered by greater intensities, but it is there blinking its own unique message. It reassures the doubters that the individual does make a difference.

Its illumination is empowered by an unusual element of coincidence. Serving in the German Infantry as an interpreter, Willi Winger was arrested by the American troops on May 15, 1945. He and his family arrived in Bismarck, North Dakota, on May 15, 1952. And he and his wife became naturalized citizens of America on May 15, 1957. The uncanny occurrence of these dates is cause for some serious speculation about the guiding force influencing the lives of the Wingers.

Added to that is the information documented by James Bacque, over forty years later, that Bad Kreuznach was a prisoner camp where Wachtmeister Winger could easily have been listed in the unexplained category of *Other Losses*.

The Winger years are uniquely and ironically theirs. A tiny genesis glow in Rumania, kindled on an Easter Sunday of 1921, came to the heartland of America and emits an ironic point of light.

Author's Notes

This book was well on its way when the book *Other Losses* by James Bacque was called to my attention by Harry Delker. I located a paperback copy in Lethbridge, Canada, while vacationing. With a mixture of awe and dismay I read the extremely well-documented pages and realized that Willi Winger had been a survivor of Bad Kreuznach, an American prisoner of war camp in Germany after World War II, without knowing that millions had died under conditions not allowed by the Geneva Convention.

In the Prologue, Dr. Delker explains in detail how this information came to be known to the public. In 1989 the *Twin Cities Reader* printed a book review on *Other Losses* by Adam Platt entitled "The U. S. Contribution to the Annals of War Atrocities." (Vol. 14, Issue 45) *Other Losses* was rejected by American publishers at that time because Bacque alleged that 1 million German soldiers and civilians died as prisoners in camps operated by the Americans and French between April 1945 and January 1946. Bacque puts the blame with General Dwight D. Eisenhower and claims the policy was deliberate and not just an accident of war. Military records provide documentation for events that are appalling.

Willi Winger's experience corroborates the material from *Other Losses*. It was number three on the Canadian bestseller list during the winter of 1989 and had to be reprinted in West Germany three days after its release, according to Platt of the *Twin Cities Reader*. It was scheduled, he says, for publication across Europe and in Japan.

To survive both the American and French incarcerations makes Willi fortunate twice and because his capture was post-war his imprisonment adds to the irony of the events that led him to America.

This account means to call Willi's face out of the masses that made history during and after World War II.

—THE AUTHOR

Chronological References for Winger Life Story

1914 A brief summary of history of Europe as pertains to Rumania and Germany.

1920 Lilly Mayer Winger was born August 20.

1921 Willi Winger was born, March 27.

1932 Willi's father died; Willi was 11 years old

1938 Willi received license for cabinet making; Willi was about 18 years old.

1939 World War II began September 1. Russians came to Bessarabia.

1940 Winger and Mayer families fled to holding camps in Czechoslovakia. Willi and Lilly met and became engaged. Lilly planned to be a Home Economics teacher.

1941 Willi was drafted into German army, June 6. After Basic Training he was sent to interpreter's school in Berlin. In the fall Lilly and her parents were transported to Poland.

1942 Willi was learning to serve as an interpreter.

1943 Willi was stationed at the Command Post in Kiev when the Russians surrounded the Germans. Lilly decided for Red Cross training over Home

Economics. She took training from March to November.

1944 Willi and Lilly married on January 6. Six months later Willi was called to active duty and they were separated.

1945 In January, Lilly and her parents ran from the Communists for the second time. Siegfried was born, April 14. Later Lilly was separated from her parents.

Willi was captured by the Americans, May 15, 1945. He was held at Bad Kreuznach, sold to the French, and used as prisoner labor at Bucancy. (Buzancy)

1947 Lilly was reunited with her parents at Stutgart. They settled at Pommertsweiler.

1948 From France, Willi was allowed to visit his family at Pommerstweiler, Germany, in the spring, but he was required to return to finish out his year of "slave labor." He was released forever on October 14.

1949 Willi obtained a job at a Wasseralfeigen truck factory and later was employed by Kessler wood factory. The letter from America and invitation to come there arrived. Edgar was born, August 24.

1952 Wingers stayed at the Bremerhafen Camp while they were screened to go to America. They left Europe in March and arrived in Bismarck, North Dakota, May 15, 1952.

Willi worked for Mr. Reche, then switched to Stude Millworks; June 15, 1952 - June 15, 1959.

1954 Lilly's parents came to America and lived with them. Willi purchased a small house and remodeled it.

1955 Edith was born, May 3.

1956 Lilly's father died. He had been born at Menno, South Dakota, but had returned to Russia at age 6.

1957 On May 15, 1957, 7:00 P.M., Bismarck, North Dakota, both Willi and Lilly were naturalized.

1959 The Wingers and Lilly's mother returned to Germany for a visit.
Willi started his own cabinet business in June. Ruth was born, August 9. Wingers built their present home.

1963 Willi built up the business, now worth $135,000.

1967 Lilly's mother died.

1970 The cabinet business was now worth $400,000 and employed twelve people.

1971 Willi converted the basement of the house where he had previously had his business into an apartment and also built a six-unit apartment house.

1972 Willi was president of Faith Lutheran Church Council.

1974 Willi purchased a building for the business.

1983 The business was sold for $285,000 in October. By now fifteen persons were employed.

1986 The buyer defaulted on payments, so Willi took the business back. 1987 Willi sold inventory only, December 15.

1988 Willi retired with empty building. Champion Auto bought it later.

1989 Wingers began interviews for life story.

From left: Lilly, Harry Delker, Berneda Koller, August Ginger (also a German-Russian who survived World War II), and Willi at the Winger home in Bismarck, North Dakota, February, 1989.

Bibliography

Ferrell, Robert H., General Editor. *The Twentieth Century: An Almanac,* "Holocaust," New York: World Almanac Publications, c1985, Bison Books.

Sulzberger, C. L. *World War II.* American Heritage Library, Houghton Mifflin Co., c1966.

World Book Encyclopedia. W-X-Y-Z, Vol. 20. "World War II, Mobilization," Field Enterprises Educational Corporation, Chicago, Illinois, c1968 and W-X-Y-Z, Vol. 21. Chicago, London, Sydney, Toronto: World Book, Inc., c1990.

Ibid, "World War II, Invasion of Russia," Field Enterprises Educational Corporation, Chicago, Illinois, c1968. Theodore Ropp, contributor of this article which was reviewed by Admiral Chester W. Nimitz and General Carl Spaatz.

World Book Encyclopedia. I, Vol. 10. Chicago, London, Sydney, Toronto: World Book, Inc., c1990 and "Immigration and Emigration," I, Vol. 10, Robert Rienow, contributor of this article, State University of New York at Albany, Field Enterprises Educational Corporation, Chicago, Illinois, c1968.

World Book Encyclpedia. Q-R, Vol. 16. Chicago, London, Sydney, Toronto: World Book, Inc., c1990 and "Romania," Q-R, Vol. 16. Field Enterprises Educational Corporation, Chicago, Illinois, c1968.

APPENDIX
Abbreviated Winger Family History Chart

LILLY'S GREAT GRANDPARENTS:

Johann Schaeffer   23 Mar 1832   28 Feb 1900
Eva Hauck   9 Aug 1835   4 Feb 1902
    Married: 18 Nov 1853   Children: 8

Johann (earlier spelled Schafer) grew up in Neudorf, South Russia. Johann and Eva arrived in Baltimore, Ohio, October, 1884. They traveled by train to Menno, South Dakota, and lived at Lesterville, South Dakota (south of Menno). Four sons and three daughters arrived in the U.S. within a similar time period. Johann was a blacksmith and several of his sons and grandsons became blacksmiths.

LILLY'S GRANDPARENTS:

Magdalena Schaeffer   10 Jan 1866   est. 1938
John Mayer   26 Feb 1860   ?
    Married: 6 Jun 1866   Children: est. 9-19

They were born and married in the U.S. In 1894 they moved to Schabo, South Russia. John died before 1938. The oldest son (name unknown) remained in the U.S. and was a mechanic on a ship which sank during WWII. The only children identified to date are Nathaniel and Reinhold.

LILLY'S PARENTS:

Nathaniel Mayer   7 Aug 1888   28 Jun 1956
Clara L. Jundt   20 Mar 1888   25 Jul 1967
    Married: 4 Mar 1912   Children: 2

Nathaniel was born at Menno, South Dakota, and at age 6 moved with his parents to Schabo, South Russia. Lilly remembers her father writing to his uncle, August Schaeffer (McClusky, North Dakota) asking for a copy of Nathaniel's birth certificate so that he could produce this document when questioned by Hitler's soldiers who required this information to insure that no Jewish persons remained in the area. At the time Nathaniel was living in Markröhlitz, Saxen, (formerly East Germany).

WILLI WINGER   27 Mar 1921
LILLY MAYER   20 Aug 1920
   Married: 6 Jan 1944   Children: 4
   Sigfried   14 Apr 1945
   Edgar   24 Aug 1949
   Edith   3 May 1955
   Ruth   9 Aug 1959

The two oldest children (Sigfried and Edgar) were born in Germany. Edith and Ruth were born in Bismarck, North Dakota. Lilly's parents came to the U.S. in 1954. (Both are buried in Bismarck.) Lilly's brother, Leo, remained in Wurttemberg and currently lives in Unterkochen, Germany.

Willi was born in Sarata, Lilly in Schabo, Rumania, now South Russia. In 1952 the Wingers came to Bismarck, North Dakota, sponsored by Lilly's great uncle (August Schaeffer) and by her father's cousins, Mathilda Houstman and Adolph Schaeffer (Mathilda's brother).

WILLI'S GRANDPARENTS AND PARENTS:

Willi's grandparents immigrated from Stuttgart, Germany, to Bessarabia in 1854. Willi's parents, Johannes and Anna Winger were born in Bessarabia.

Sources: (1) "The Bertsch Book—222 years"
              by Harry A. Delker, Aberdeen, SD, 1986.
          (2) Willi and Lilly Winger, Bismarck, ND, 1993.